15- minute focus
Brief Counseling
Techniques that Work

EXECUTIVE FUNCTION

STRATEGIES TO BUILD UNDERDEVELOPED SKILLS, MAXIMIZE LEARNING, AND UNLOCK POTENTIAL

NATIONAL CENTER for
YOUTH ISSUES

Contents

Contents 4

Introduction 7

    What Led Me to Write This Book.. 8

    What Led You to This Book? 10

    21st Century Skills... 11

CHAPTER 1

Getting to Know Executive Function, the Brain, and Yourself 13

    What is Executive Function? 13

    Your Role in Building Executive Function and Shaping Healthy Brains 14

    Executive Function and Social-Emotional Learning Go Hand-in-Hand 16

    Best and Worst Learning Experiences................................ 18

    Reflection 19

    Use Neuroplasticity to Your Advantage 19

    Neurodiversity as an Opportunity 20

    Executive Function Profile 22

    Assessing Executive Function.. 29

CHAPTER 2

Executive Dysfunction and Its Impact 34

    Impact on Reading 34

    Impact on Writing... 39

    Impact on Math 43

    Impact on Relationships 46

    Impact on Time 48

    Impact on Transitions 53

    Impact on Homework 54

    Impact on Notetaking 55

    Foundational Strategies 56

15-MINUTE FOCUS
Executive Function: Strategies to Build Underdeveloped Skills,
Maximize Learning, and Unlock Potential

Praise for

Executive Function
Strategies to Build Underdeveloped Skills, Maximize Learning, and Unlock Potential

Delve into the depths of Noel Foy's great book on executive functioning. A critical and complex notion made simpler and more practical for every educator.

John Hattie

Author of the *Visible Learning Series*, Emeritus Laureate Professor at the Graduate School of Education, University of Melbourne, Australia

Foy pulls together an impressive amount of information in a readable, useable format. Readers can dive in and immediately learn concrete ways to support and build EF.

Lynn Lyons

Psychotherapist, Anxiety Specialist, and Author

Noel Foy's book is an invaluable resource for both teachers and parents! Her user-friendly guide provides a plethora of practical strategies and tips for building executive function processes.

Lynn Meltzer, Ph.D.

President and Director, Research ILD (Research Institute for Learning and Development)

If you are eager to learn more about EF and how to facilitate its use by children and your life or profession, this book will be a valuable resource.

Jack A Naglieri, Ph.D.

Foy provides a user-friendly guide for educators and caregivers that identifies many different ways in which EF challenges can impact students and offers practical strategies and tips that can be used in real time to support and--just as importantly--encourage students in building their EF skills.

Sarah Ward, M.S. CCC-SLP

Co-Author of *360 Thinking Method*

Dedication

For Tammy—who knew that a random roommate assignment of two "rookie" teachers would lead to a life-long friendship. No matter our geographical distance, you will always remain in my heart and continue to inspire me.

Funding to help underwrite the development of the *15-Minute Focus* series has been generously provided by:

PASTORAL INSTITUTE

SARAH T. BUTLER CHILDREN'S CENTER COLUMBUS, GEORGIA

The Sarah T. Butler Children's Center at the Pastoral Institute of Columbus, Georgia is dedicated to the mental health and well-being of children ages 1-18. This center provides comprehensive services that span psychological testing, intervention, therapy groups, and counseling. In all our activities we seek to inspire growth through faith, hope, and love.

Duplication and Copyright

NCYI titles may be purchased in bulk at special discounts for educational, business, fundraising, or promotional use. For more information, please email sales@ncyi.org.

NATIONAL CENTER for
YOUTH ISSUES

P.O. Box 22185
Chattanooga, TN 37422-2185
423.899.5714 • 866.318.6294
fax: 423.899.4547 • www.ncyi.org

Print: 9781953945938
eBook: 9781953945945
Library of Congress Control Number: 2024948758
© 2024 National Center for Youth Issues, Chattanooga, TN
All rights reserved.
Written by: Noel Foy
Published by National Center for Youth Issues
Printed in the U.S.A. • February 2025

Third party links are accurate at the time of publication, but may change over time.

The information in this book is designed to provide helpful information on the subjects discussed and is not intended to be used, nor should it be used, to diagnose or treat any mental health or medical condition. For diagnosis or treatment of any mental health or medical issue, consult a licensed counselor, psychologist, or physician. The publisher and author are not responsible for any specific mental or physical health needs that may require medical supervision, and are not liable for any damages or negative consequences from any treatment, action, application, or preparation, to any person reading or following the information in this book. References are provided for informational purposes only and do not constitute endorsement of any websites or other sources.

CHAPTER 3

When Stress Goes Up, Learning Goes Down 61

Quick Mind/Body Check with 4/6 Breathing 62

Cultivate Low Threat, High-Learning Environments 63

Teach Kids About the Stress Response 64

Not All Stress is Bad.. 70

What to Say to Lower Stress: Quick Language Scaffolds...................... 70

Building Better Communication and Mindsets............................... 73

What to Do to Decrease Stress: Quick Resets 76

Common Behaviors: "What Are They Telling Us?"................................. 80

CHAPTER 4

More of Them, Less of You.. 83

Resist the Urge to Be Kids' Pre-Frontal Cortex 83

Ways to Boost Metacognition... 85

Make Learning Environments "No PEE Zones" 89

Reduce Teacher Talk, Increase Student Learning................................. 90

Retrieval Strategies: How To Be a "Golden" Retriever........................... 92

Self-Monitoring.. 95

CHAPTER 5

Brain-Appealing, Dopamine-Friendly Environments............................. 100

Be a Dopamine Conduit.. 100

Strategies to Internalize Routines 109

Conclusion 118

Endnotes 120

Resources 123

Websites.. 123

Videos.. 125

Articles/Blogs.. 125

Podcasts.. 127

Tools 127

Apps... 128

Books 128

E-Book.. 129

Acknowledgements.. 130

About the Author 131

Other Books by Noel.. 131

A Brief Look at Noel's Sessions 132

15-Minute Focus Series 133

About NCYI 136

**See page 130 for information about
Downloadable Resources and Templates**

Introduction

In the middle of difficulty lies opportunity.
Albert Einstein

Have you ever been expected to complete a task but didn't have the necessary skills to do so…*yet?*

For example, if I suddenly switched from writing in English to Spanish, it would be difficult for you to comprehend this book unless you already knew how to read Spanish.

Let's consider a different challenge.

Say I asked you to stop reading and juggle seven balls in the air.

That's right, juggle seven balls. How's it going so far?

Not so well? What's holding you back?

Maybe you're thinking, "I don't know how to start," "I can't juggle," or "This is too hard." Perhaps you're attempting to toss a few balls in the air, but they keep falling to the ground. You might feel frustrated, anxious, or overwhelmed. Unless, of course, you already know how to juggle.

You might wonder, "What a goofy challenge. What's the point?"

I hope it gives you a sense of what it feels like to lack the skills you need to begin a task, stick with it when it's hard, and complete it.

If you don't know how to juggle, expecting you to do so *on demand* with success and efficiency will be stressful and unrealistic.

Yet, we ask this daily of many students with neurodiversity or underdeveloped executive function.

Imagine needing to know how to juggle for most everything you do—at home, in school, relationships, and jobs. Picture being told you're smart and capable, yet you struggle with "keeping several balls in the air," "showing what you know," or "putting it all together." Feel the frustration, disappointment, and discouragement you'd likely experience. No wonder many kids consider school a stressful place where they don't feel successful.

What Led Me to Write This Book

By the time my sons reached 4th grade, the spark they once had for school was barely a flicker. When asked, "How was school?" "Boring" was the daily refrain. "What did you learn?" "Nothing" was the typical response. School seemed stressful for my kids, but I wasn't sure why. I was particularly frustrated because *I was a teacher*—a special educator to boot. Yet, I felt unequipped to find the root of the problem and believed I had fallen short as an educator and parent. *Why* did my kids love learning but dislike school?

Over the years**, I discovered they were not alone.**

As I evolved into an anxiety/executive function coach and neuroeducation consultant, I was struck by what I observed in many classrooms across the county: an increase of students in stressful emotional states—anxiety, frustration, anger, boredom, and a lack of relevance to what they were learning—which caused them to act out or zone out.

I found myself in conversations with teachers, counselors, and parents who expressed concern that many kids lacked focus, motivation, resilience, self-regulation, and self-awareness.

What was going on?

It wasn't until I attended a Learning and the Brain Conference that I started to get answers. A breakthrough moment was becoming aware of the impact of stress on learning. High states of stress can hijack **executive function (EF)**: brain functions that guide thinking and behavior for learning, achieving goals, juggling demands, and navigating life. When EF goes "offline," we don't focus, produce, or perform well. This pivotal discovery, along with an understanding of how the brain best learns and responds, was absent from my teacher training.

Armed with this new knowledge, I realized stress inhibited the learning, productivity, efficiency, and overall success of many students, my sons included, yet they (and most adults in their lives) were unaware of its impact. I also discovered that:

- Many aspiring teachers and counselors at the undergraduate level lack practical training in EF, behavioral principles, neurodivergence, or mental health, yet they are expected to know how to intervene and respond to students with these challenges.

- Many students do not learn about EF, the brain, and how it develops and learns best, yet instructional practices often omit metacognitive, brain-appealing approaches.
- Employers seek candidates with strong EF, yet students receive little *explicit* instruction on how their brains work and react to stressors.

While some schools offer professional development in these areas, I believe these topics are grossly underrepresented, leaving many educators and parents to figure things out on their own. To date, teacher preparation doesn't adequately reflect exciting neuroscience discoveries and rapid changes in our world. Anxiety and depression were well on the rise before the pandemic, and today's classrooms include a substantial mix of students with neurodiversity and mental health challenges. Consequently, teachers, counselors, and parents need quick, effective tools to reduce stress, enhance instruction, boost EF, and help kids experience more success, connection, meaning, and fulfillment in school and life. Without this toolbox, I believe we're insufficiently equipped to address the needs of the kids in front of us and prepare them for life's challenges.

I'm not okay with that, and since you are reading this book, I suspect you aren't either.

My increased understanding of executive function compelled me to shift my career track…and to write this book. Employing a synthesis of research-based findings and strategies I use with kids and adults in my one-on-one and group coaching sessions, I aspire to deepen your understanding of EF by going beyond theories to provide real-time solutions to common challenges associated with executive dysfunction. Besides helping your students start tasks, complete homework, and develop organizational systems to succeed in school, I aim to empower you—and them—with key strategies, language frames, brain discoveries, and skills to function well *in life*. I've time-tested the principles and strategies in this book for transfer use in school, home, athletic, and work settings. While not a formal diagnostic tool, the chapters ahead can increase the quality of teacher preparation, classroom instruction, support services, parent education, and professional learning.

What Led You to This Book?

If you picked up this book, you're probably curious to learn more about EF and how to facilitate its development in your life or profession. Perhaps you see this as an opportunity to better teach and support neurodiverse learners. Whatever the case, thank you for your curiosity in these topics! It's quite a juggling act working with "all kinds of minds."

You might be dealing with individuals who:

- don't know how to start an assignment or can't find their assignment
- check out or freak out in class
- resist transitioning to the next task
- cave at the first sign of difficulty or think it's cooler to say "this is stupid" than ask for help
- are chronically late or unprepared yet seem unaware of the consequences of their decisions

Sound familiar? These are the students I work with the most. I believe their unproductive patterns reflect underdeveloped cognitive, social, and emotional skills, not an inability or unwillingness to learn. If you know students who procrastinate, struggle to pay attention, forget homework, miss appointments, or lack consistent effort, their behavior may lead you to conclude they don't care. I have found that's not the case.

My sons' boredom in school and the one-size-fits-all way they were taught led to increased stress and decreased learning, and their experience is only one of countless examples I could offer. We as educators must appreciate the uniqueness of each brain and its ability to think, process, learn, and interact with the world. We each possess strengths and challenges, and we all offer valuable variations in how our brains work, whether it's an ability to hyperfocus, see the "big picture," or think outside the box. Consequently, we must teach and support kids in ways that maximize their learning and EF. This book attempts to fulfill that aim, and I'm so glad you're joining me on this journey!

In the following chapters, you'll learn how to:

- build better brains and learning environments
- identify EF strengths, challenges, and the impact of stress

- use quick, practical tools to support goal setting, planning, organization, task initiation, transitions, routines, working memory, time management, self-regulation, and self-monitoring
- implement simple, metacognitive applications that decrease stress and behavior issues and boost learning, engagement, and a productive mindset for success in and beyond school.

Given the intent of this book, many strategies can be done in less than 15 minutes and are designed to seamlessly embed into any environment, strengthening *multiple* EF issues at the same time instead of targeting them in isolation. You can read the book and start implementing on the same day!

21st Century Skills

We rely on EF and a mix of cognitive, social, and emotional skills to succeed in school, relationships, careers, and life. Research supports that emotional intelligence (EQ), which includes an ability to identify and manage emotions and work well with others, are predictors of success. Daniel Goleman, author of *Emotional Intelligence*, discovered EQ accounts for 80% of career success and sets apart notable leaders from mediocre ones. Goleman's study of approximately 200 executives found EQ doubly important than IQ and technical expertise in fueling performance. At top levels, EQ distinguished 90% of the "best from the rest."[1]

EF, social and emotional learning (SEL), and EQ comprise some of the most sought-after skills by employers, including many of the skills mentioned in the Top Skills of 2023 chart and those listed below:

- Critical thinking (decision making, analytical thinking, creativity)
- Task initiation
- Self-awareness
- Empathy
- Self-regulation
- Collaboration
- Effort/growth mindset (motivation, overcoming obstacles, feedback receptivity)
- Time management/organization
- Adaptability/flexible thinking
- Written/oral communication

Top 10 Skills of 2023

1.	Analytical Thinking		6.	Technological Literacy
2.	Creative Thinking		7.	Dependability and Attention to Detail
3.	Resilience, Flexibility, and Agility		8.	Empathy and Active Listening
4.	Motivation and Self-Awareness		9.	Leadership and Social Influence
5.	Curiosity and Lifelong Learning		10.	Quality Control

Type of Skill

Cognitive Skills   Self-Efficacy   Management Skills   Technology Skills   Working With Others

Source: World Economic Forum, Future of Jobs Report, 2023

Are you satisfied with the level of preparation students currently receive in these areas?

To be honest, I'm not. I believe we can do better.

I believe we have an opportunity to shape kids' brains in amazing ways. We can facilitate life-changing outcomes by helping them develop strong EF and productive habits within the context of their daily learning and responsibilities.

I believe *all* students want to learn and succeed.

I believe students' gaps in Executive Function, Social-Emotional Learning, and Emotional Intelligence *can* and *will* improve with proper skill-building. Many just aren't strong in these areas…*YET!*

I have seen firsthand how decreasing stress and bolstering EF can transform lives, elevating learning, motivation, confidence, self-worth, and students' ability to become efficient, self-directed, critical thinkers.

I'm excited to support you in your effort to do just that. I've got your back!

Noel

Getting to Know Executive Function, the Brain, and Yourself

1

The neurons that fire together, wire together.

Donald Hebb

What is Executive Function?

When someone mentions executive function (EF), what comes to mind? In my experience, many people are familiar with the term but aren't clear about its scope or impact on daily life. Some people with EF challenges have difficulty regulating emotions or impulses. Others have trouble setting goals, managing time, or remembering what they need to do. For some, all the above and more apply.

I admit, learning about EF can be tricky, starting with its definition. A quick internet search leads to multiple variations, including:

- …a self-directed set of actions intended to alter a future outcome such as a goal. (Russell Barkley, Ph. D., leader in psychology and ADHD/ADD research)[2]
- "…a diverse group of cognitive processes that act in a coordinated way to direct perception, emotion, thought and action" and …"are responsible for a person's ability to engage in purposeful, organized, strategic, self-regulated, goal-directed behavior." (George McCloskey, Ph.D., author of McCloskey Executive Function Scales MEFS)[3]
- "…executive skills allow us to organize our behavior over time

and override immediate demands in favor of longer-term goals." (Peg Dawson and Richard Guare, authors of the *Smart But Scattered* series)[4]

While definitions, semantics, and models vary, most field experts agree that EF involves self-driven, goal-directed behavior that guides future direction and utilizes the highest aspects of brain functions to organize, prioritize, and manage daily life. Often associated with a set of skills that make a chief executive officer successful, EF allows us to juggle various responsibilities, interact with others, regulate emotions, make adjustments to achieve a desired result, and get stuff done. As psychologist and researcher Jack Naglieri says, "It's the thinking a person uses to decide how to achieve any goal, which includes self-monitoring and self-corrections as needed."[5]

To better understand how EF works in an integrated fashion, imagine how an orchestra conductor cues certain musicians to bring their instruments "online" at precise times throughout a song, coordinating them in a synced fashion and directing how to proceed with the wave of a baton. If the musicians don't work together and play when signaled, the music may be a mix of discordant sounds rather than a cohesive piece. In the same way, we must learn how to be conductors of our own brains and teach kids how to do the same!

Your Role in Building Executive Function and Shaping Healthy Brains

EF development begins shortly after birth and is influenced by a child's genes and environment. If a parent has ADHD or a child grows up in a home with trauma or lead exposure, the risk of EF challenges may be increased. With the first three years of life being the most rapid period of brain development and adolescence being the second most significant, we as educators, parents, caregivers, support professionals, and coaches play critical roles in building EF and healthy brains.[6]

By preschool, students build EF by learning how to take turns, follow routines, remember directions, transition to new activities, keep emotions in check, and adjust their approach to a task if their current method isn't working. In elementary school, skill-building continues by doing simple chores, completing homework, and following classroom norms. During the middle school years, transitions become faster and more frequent, with students practicing self-regulation and developing systems for notetaking, homework, and long-term projects. By high school, students' demands increase to meet deadlines, manage time, set goals, and inhibit risky behaviors. If students receive regular practice in these areas, EF improves rapidly throughout their childhood and adolescent years. By late adolescence, "adult" networks are fairly formed but continue developing well into the twenties.

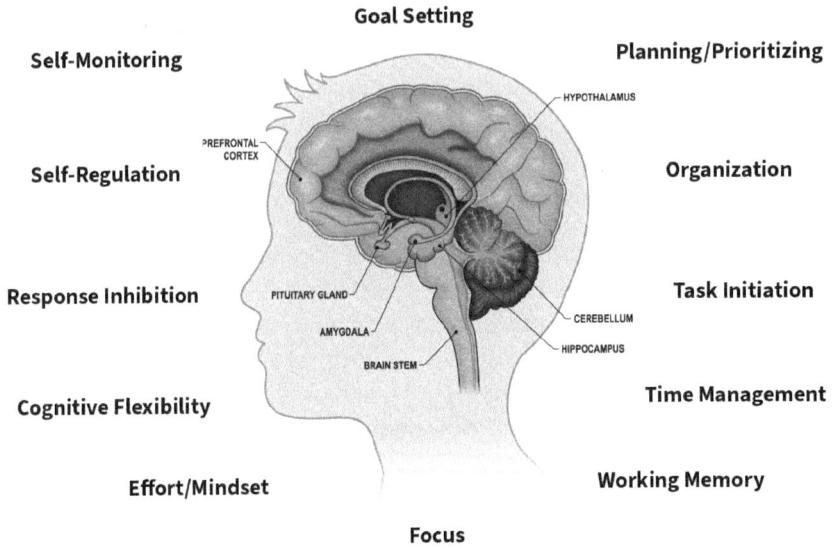

Judy Willis, a neurologist and former classroom teacher, reminds us, "Neural networks that control executive function develop in the pre-frontal cortex and do so most profoundly during school years."[7] The pre-frontal cortex is prime real estate for executive function (though the last part of the brain to mature) and interacts with other brain regions to control, direct, and manage behavior.[8] For this part of the brain to develop sufficiently, students need consistent opportunities to develop these neural networks, which makes your job so important!

Executive Function and Social-Emotional Learning Go Hand-in-Hand

We as educators must intertwine EF, academic competencies, and Social and Emotional Learning (SEL) in kids' environments from the onset, helping them name and express emotions productively, learn constructive self-talk, and feel safe to make mistakes. Aspects of SEL include: self-awareness, social awareness, self-management, decision making, and relationship skills. These building blocks strengthen EF and develop emotional intelligence (EQ).[9] Research supports a strong link between EF, SEL, and success in school, social interactions, jobs, and life. "SEL not only improves achievement by an average of 11 percentile points, but it also increases pro-social behaviors (such as kindness, sharing, and empathy), improves student attitudes toward school, and reduces depression and stress among students."[10]

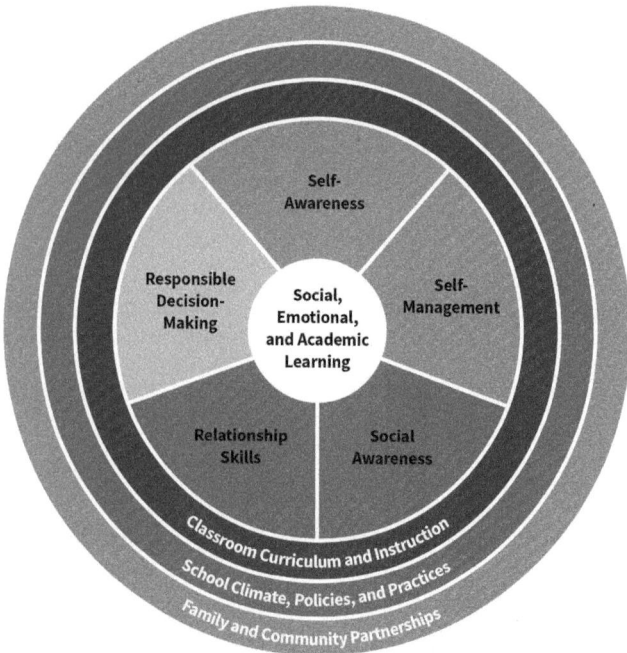

Source: http://secondaryguide.casel.org/casel

Students with underdeveloped EF often need support with SEL. They might experience high stress and academic challenges, which can lead to doubting themselves as learners and viewing school in a negative light. This affects their self-talk, mindset, motivation, decision making, and approach to life. Kids may be sent to the principal more frequently when they struggle with impulsivity, distractibility, controlling emotions, interacting with peers, or sticking to routines. A trip to the main office can result in missed class time, falling behind, talking to themselves harshly, and acting out. A downward cycle can begin.

Some of my biggest pet peeves are when I hear students described as lazy, able to "turn it on when they want to," or "will never change." Kids take these damaging, unproductive labels to heart. Some students have missed pivotal opportunities to build EF, live with undiagnosed ADHD, or are dealing with trauma, learning challenges, mental health issues, or a mix of stressors. Executive dysfunction is not a measurement of character, nor does it mean someone isn't intelligent or capable; it's often quite the opposite! However, being smart is not enough. A student might be bright but a slow processor. They may comprehend a concept but not know how to start an essay, delay gratification, or work well in a group.

Emotions also impact learning—for better or worse. In the learning process, we experience emotions that lay the foundation for healthy or unhealthy narratives about ourselves. If students have repeated negative experiences, a stress chemical called cortisol increases, which can lead to behavior issues (i.e., avoiding challenges, reluctance to learning). What these kids might remember about being in school or a class is that it bored them or they couldn't do the work. However, learning that elicits productive thoughts, emotions, and multi-sensory experiences develops efficient networks that boost the retrieval of information, and builds confidence and resilience. As Judy Willis reinforces, "The stimulation during the ages of their rapid development strongly influences social-emotional control and the highest thinking skill sets that today's students will carry with them as they leave school and become adults."[11]

Learning... ...can go either way.

Your Turn!

Think about any students who have dealt with repeated negative learning experiences and tell themselves unhealthy narratives.

Throughout this book, you will learn ways to support these students and help them re-write "their story."

Best and Worst Learning Experiences

To better understand the connection of emotion to learning, reflect on the questions in the **Best and Worst Learning Experiences Worksheet**, which is based on an activity from a Judy Willis workshop. Answer the questions yourself first and then ask your student(s) to do so. Let kids share their answers because you'll hear some interesting insights.

NAME: _____   DATE: _____

Best and Worst Learning Experiences

1. Think of some of your worst learning experiences (i.e. academics, sports, or extra-curriculars). List 2-3.
_____
_____
_____

2. How would you describe your emotions in these situations?
_____
_____
_____

3. Think of some of your best learning experiences. List 2-3.
_____
_____
_____

4. What were your emotions during these experiences?
_____
_____
_____

15-Minute Focus: Executive Function: Strategies to Build Underdeveloped Skills, Maximize Learning, and Unlock Potential by Noel Foy
© National Center for Youth Issues www.ncyi.org

Reflection

Notice any patterns? You likely felt safe, interested, engaged, and appropriately challenged during your best learning experiences. That's how I felt when I learned how to drive a stick shift, play tennis, and craft a story. However, chemistry and biology classes topped my worst learning experiences. I was overwhelmed by the pace and felt frustrated by my lack of understanding, but I was afraid to ask questions for fear of looking inept or unprepared. Additionally, I didn't see the relevance to what I was learning (ironically, science is a foundation of my work today) and was bored by the dry, one-size-fits-all lecture approach.

What I didn't know then but know now is my EF was hijacked during these stressful moments, making it difficult to pay attention, remember what the teacher said, and absorb information needed for later retrieval. The stressful states I experienced as a student also challenge many kids today and interfere with their learning and success. *But it doesn't have to stay that way.* By integrating the information, tools, and strategies in this book, you can help kids build better brains and environments in which to flourish.

Use Neuroplasticity to Your Advantage

Kids need to know about EF and its connection to neuroplasticity, the brain's ability to grow and change based on how it's used. We must teach kids that EF neural networks begin to form in infancy and get stronger and faster with intentional practice and repeated activation of skill-building habits and strategies. If these networks don't receive regular reinforcement, under-activated neurons will prune away, and the neural pathways needed to develop EF will be weak.[12]

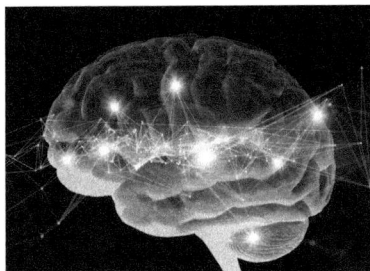

We want students to know they are works in progress. "Brains are built, not born!"[13] By teaching kids about neuroplasticity, they discover the connection of effort to progress. Strengthening neural connections is similar to going to the gym or learning a new skill (i.e., how to ride a bike or play an instrument). Through repetition, practice, and feedback, they'll start to see improvement that would not occur by learning a skill sporadically, repeating improper form, or ignoring mistakes. The same goes for executive function and neuroplasticity—kids must regularly "flex these muscles" to build skills.

To get kids thinking about change and growth, ask them questions such as:

- Do you believe in change? Why/why not?
- What are some habits you've changed in your life? What about ways of thinking?
- What's something you couldn't do previously that you can do now? How'd you get good at it?

These types of questions can lead to interesting discussions. When I teach kids that their brains become stronger by building new skills and correcting mistakes, they find this eye-opening and become more receptive to adjusting, taking academic risks, and seeking help. Many even begin to view neuroplasticity as their newfound "superpower!"

Neurodiversity as an Opportunity

Your students may learn in completely different ways than you, and that's okay! Some students like to write down their thoughts, while others prefer to draw or discuss them, which is why multi-sensory instruction is so important. We learn from our senses, so we as educators can take advantage of them and provide students with different opportunities to access and process information.

Neurodiversity reminds us that we all possess our own strengths and "ways of getting there." We want neurodiverse learners to value their differences and choose classes, activities, and careers that suit them. Think of those who have done so: Animal behavioralist Temple Grandin (autism), Shark Tank judge Barbara Corcoran (dyslexia), Olympian Michael Phelps (ADHD), and business magnate Richard Branson (dyslexia, ADHD). Their successes highlight the need to challenge perceptions about those who don't learn in traditional ways.

While genes play a role in inheriting conditions such as ADHD, dyslexia, dyscalculia, or anxiety, the quality of school experiences, interventions, and accommodations also shape kids' brains by either building or inhibiting executive function development. For students with ADHD, their frontal cortex brain regions (important for attention, planning, and decision making) mature approximately 2-3 years behind their peers, so a 16-year old's EF age is about 13.[14] Boys are more likely than girls to be diagnosed as having ADHD, with girls scoring higher on executive function scales than boys, especially regarding social and emotional skills. However, girls are more likely to go undiagnosed.[15] Children with Autism Spectrum Disorder (ASD) often experience EF and SEL gaps, particularly with planning, cognitive flexibility, inhibition, social interactions, and identifying and managing emotions (in themselves and others).[16] Whether these students take medications to manage their symptoms or not, they will need an EF toolbox to juggle life's competing demands. Educators play key roles in helping kids fill that toolkit, especially since they spend a significant amount of time with kids, second only to parents.

Executive Function Profile

In this section, you will get a better sense of the scope of executive function, its effect on daily life and how to build underdeveloped skills by:

- understanding each executive skill and its common patterns (**Informal Executive Function Inventory**)
- rating current ability in each area (**Executive Function Questionnaire**)
- categorizing strengths, inconsistencies, and challenges (**Getting to Know Me Worksheet)**
- formulating a plan to improve targeted areas (**Skill Building Plan**)

Note: The inventory, questionnaire, and worksheet may be used as self-report tools in middle school (and up) or to determine the needs of a student. For the **Skill Building Plan**, it is important to specify who will teach the skills and strategies (i.e., teacher, counselor, parent, support professional, etc.). When I work with students, I model the strategies via a think aloud technique and then segue to guided practice before asking them to apply independently.

INFORMAL EXECUTIVE FUNCTION INVENTORY

EXECUTIVE SKILL	DEFINITION	PATTERNS
Goal Setting	The ability to set, initiate, and complete a goal	**Strength:** I tend to set realistic short/long-term goals and see them through, even if obstacles arise. **Challenge:** I'm more focused on the "here and now," versus future plans or carrying out goals.

EXECUTIVE SKILL	DEFINITION	PATTERNS
Planning/ Prioritizing	The ability to visualize a plan and steps to complete a goal	**Strength:** When I start something, I typically have a plan, break it into chunks, and prioritize what's important. **Challenge:** I often lack a plan, get lost in the details or non-essentials, and have difficulty with lots of info/steps or where to start.
Organization	The ability to order and keep track of materials, items, or information needed for a task	**Strength:** I arrive at destinations with what's needed, I dislike clutter, and I have a system for organizing things/information. **Challenge**: Things or information tend to pile up without a system, and I might put items down randomly or forget what I need.
Task Initiation	The ability to start a task in a timely, efficient way	**Strength:** I don't need external reminders or motivators to start tasks. **Challenge:** I tend to put things off until the last minute, often resulting in missed deadlines or feeling overwhelmed.
Time Management	The ability to estimate how long something might take and allocate time to finish within constraints/deadlines	**Strength:** I arrive on time for obligations and budget the time needed to complete tasks. **Challenge:** I typically under or over-estimate how long something takes and don't use planning tools.

EXECUTIVE SKILL	DEFINITION	PATTERNS
Working Memory	The ability to retain information (i.e., numbers, names, steps, directions) to complete a task/activity	**Strength:** I'm good at remembering directions, details, belongings, tasks, etc. **Challenge:** I often forget items, appointments, details, steps, or information needed to complete a task.
Focus	The ability to pay attention and sustain focus, even when distracted or bored	**Strength:** I can focus on tasks, filter out distractions, and get stuff done, even if it's tedious or boring. **Challenge:** I have trouble staying attentive, following through, and sticking with tasks if interrupted or distracted.
Effort/Mindset	The ability to show effort and persevere on tasks with a productive attitude that overcomes challenges, sticks with things when hard, and is open to feedback/growth	**Strength:** I can delay gratification, put in steady effort, and be receptive to feedback, even when things are challenging. **Challenge:** I might avoid asking for help, undervalue effort and/or practice, and quit when a task becomes difficult.
Cognitive Flexibility	The ability to switch between tasks, adjust to setbacks, mistakes, changes in the plan, or new routines/perspectives	**Strength:** I transition smoothly between tasks and "go with the flow," even when plans change. **Challenge:** I tend to lack a Plan B and struggle to switch tasks or adjust to changes in approach, location, or plans.

EXECUTIVE SKILL	DEFINITION	PATTERNS
Response Inhibition	The ability to delay gratification, think before acting, and resist the urge to react before assessing a situation	**Strength:** I think through choices and consequences and how my words and actions can help or hurt things. **Challenge:** I might blurt out my words, be impulsive, or make snap judgments.
Self-Regulation	The ability to express emotions appropriately (even when things get tough) while completing a task or pursuing a goal	**Strength:** I manage emotions in productive ways and know how to "pump the brakes" when stressed. **Challenge:** My emotions often get the best of me, and I might overreact to minor setbacks or challenges.
Self-Monitoring	The ability to learn from past mistakes, make necessary adjustments, and be aware of my progress with a task or skill.	**Strength:** I take stock to see how things are progressing and make adjustments or seek help (if needed). **Challenge:** I often push through tasks, don't stop to make tweaks, or communicate what's going on, even if it isn't progressing well.

Becoming aware of the above patterns can help explain why some individuals are drawn to certain tasks or subjects, avoid others, or find some situations enjoyable but get frustrated with others. Some people may discover they're good at a few or many of these skills. Others might be confused as to why some people aren't proficient in them. Or, perhaps they empathize with their challenges.

It's normal to be adept at some skills and not so great at others. If you, a student, or loved one isn't strong in all these areas, fear not! Most of us have some EF gaps that need improvement. One of mine is underestimating how long a task or project takes to finish—like this book!

Now that you have a better understanding of common patterns, use the following **Executive Function Questionnaire** to rate your current ability of each skill:

NAME: _____   DATE: _____

Executive Function Questionnaire

Rate your current ability with these skills. Do you usually, sometimes, or rarely exhibit each skill?

	Usually	Sometimes	Rarely
GOAL SETTING			
• Set realistic goals?			
• See goals through to completion?			
PLANNING/PRIORITIZING			
• Use a planner to schedule when to do tasks?			
• Chunk assignments/tasks?			
• Plan steps to complete assignments/tasks?			
• Prioritize what's most important?			
ORGANIZATION			
Have a system for organizing/keeping track of:			
• things?			
• personal space?			
• information?			
TASK INITIATION			
• Initiate tasks/plan in a timely manner (vs. procrastinate)?			
• Communicate necessary information?			
TIME MANAGEMENT			
• Arrive on time for commitments?			
• Estimate and budget time to complete tasks?			
WORKING MEMORY			
• Remember important information/details?			
• Follow directions/steps?			
FOCUS			
• Stay attentive/focused (avoid distractions)?			
• Follow through with tasks/commitments?			

	Usually	Sometimes	Rarely
EFFORT/MINDSET			
• Ask for help?			
• Maintain perseverance and stamina to finish tasks?			
• Overcome obstacles or setbacks?			
COGNITIVE FLEXIBILITY			
• Adapt well to change and transitions?			
• Try other solutions when stuck?			
RESPONSE INHIBITION			
• Think through the consequences of actions and comments on others?			
• Blurt, "cross the line," or show impulsivity?			
SELF-REGULATION			
• Manage stress and express emotions in productive ways (vs. act out, avoid challenges, or "freeze" on performance-based tasks)?			
SELF-MONITORING			
• Draw on past approaches for what has/has not worked?			
• Self-monitor progress and make changes when needed?			

Additionally, you can explore other strengths, inconsistencies, or challenges regarding:

- Reading, Writing, Math, Science, History, Technology, etc.
- Music
- Sports
- Homework
- Taking tests

Next, categorize the information you gathered from the **Executive Function Questionnaire** and the above list into the **Getting to Know Me Worksheet**. Here's an example:

NAME: _____   DATE: _____

Getting To Know Me (Example)

Fill in the chart with your strengths, inconsistences, and challenges.

STRENGTHS

Sports	Technology
Music	Setting Goals
Asking for help	

INCONSISTENCIES

Mindset (depends on task)	Time Management
Homework/Tests (situational)	Self-monitoring
Organization	Focus (if interested in the topic)
Planning/Prioritizing	

CHALLENGES

Working Memory	Response Inhibition
Task Initiation w/writing	Self-regulation
Cognitive Flexibility	

15-Minute Focus: Executive Function: Strategies to Build Underdeveloped Skills, Maximize Learning, and Unlock Potential by Neal Fay
© National Center for Youth Issues www.ncyi.org

To build metacognitive awareness, students need to understand their strengths, challenges, and inconsistencies, which may be impacted by their environment or interest in a subject or skill. We want kids to celebrate and pursue their strengths but also be aware and willing to build underdeveloped skills.

What's next? Including a student in the process as much as possible, complete the first three steps of the **Skill Building Plan** by targeting an underdeveloped skill or two (from the **Challenges** section of the **Getting to Know Me Worksheet**). Help the student set an achievable goal and state its relevance. As you read the upcoming chapters, you can add information, strategies, and activities to the plan. Keep in mind that building a skill rarely develops in isolation. Bolstering one skill often improves others (i.e., task initiation can support planning and time management), as shown in the following example:

NAME: _____   DATE: _____

Skill Building Plan (Example)

Underdeveloped Skill(s) to Improve: Time/Planning, Task Initiation

Set an Achievable Goal: Chunk and schedule this week's assignments in planner's time slots

How is this goal personally relevant? Will feel less stress, more in control; no late penalties

Steps to Reaching this Goal:	Visual/verbal cues to help:
1. Say out loud, "I am a time planner and task starter." 2. Have planner, assignments/syllabi, laptop available. 3. Use the Pomodoro Technique to start my goal. (Repeat Pomodoro, if necessary)	• Future Glasses (i.e. When I picture myself doing this goal, what do I see?) • Analog Clock • "The brain that does the work does the learning!"

Obstacles/Solutions to Reaching this Goal:	As you practice this skill, evaluate:
If I'm tempted to procrastinate (obstacle), then I will remind myself I can't form better habits without practicing these new approaches (solution). If I lack motivation (obstacle), then I will raise my dopamine with a brief music/movement break (solution).	**What's working:** Future Glasses, Pomodoro, productive self-talk, less stress **What's not working:** Having my phone nearby **What adjustments to make:** Put phone in another room (if home) or in my bag

15-Minute Focus: Executive Function, Strategies to Build Underdeveloped Skills, Maximize Learning, and Unlock Potential by Noel Foy
© National Center for Youth Issues www.ncyi.org

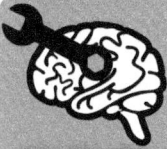

Make It Relevant

You probably feel more motivated, invested, and engaged when a topic or skill is relevant to you.

Your students are no different, and here's why: the brain likes relevance!

Make real life connections of topics and goals to situations that interest kids. For example, kids need to be aware that people with good EF who read and write well experience greater academic success, land better paying jobs, and make more money in their lifetime. Even if kids find these outcomes motivating, incentives themselves won't build their executive function. Skill building takes time, effort, and practice, which is why you might consider incorporating the application of good EF into your grading systems.

Assessing Executive Function

Students can demonstrate a range of EF challenges, which can be impacted by ADHD, anxiety, depression, autism, trauma, or a traumatic brain injury. If you suspect a student needs to be assessed, reach out to parents, teachers, and the school psychologist. An evaluation will reveal strengths and areas of need, and it lays the groundwork for a support plan. A referral may be needed to a Special Education or Student Assistance Team (IEP, Section 504), or outside support.

Be forewarned. Just as there isn't one definition for EF, there isn't one assessment process, test, or tool, and may include a mix of:

Informal Assessments

- **Case history**: feedback from teachers, parents, and those who know the child well, including medical history, strengths and needs for each executive skill, when EF challenges are most noticeable, what previous interventions have worked (or not), and receptivity of people in child's life to make changes in approach/environment

- **Work samples**: tests, writing samples, child's backpack, and workspace
- **Classroom observations:** observing the child within daily school demands, what is happening in class, antecedents, and how a child (and those around them) responds to skill gaps
- **Questionnaires/rating scales**

Formal Assessments

A neuropsychological evaluation includes a mix of tests, questionnaires, interviews, and observations that reveal the student's cognitive ability, strengths/gaps, academic and processing skills, and approach to specific tasks.

Student Story

Brendan, a high school junior, found school boring and was mystified by friends who said they liked it. Though Brendan did well in classes that interested him, he had trouble focusing on subjects that lacked relevance to his life.

Brendan typically did enough work "to get by," although he'd often miss directions and deadlines, struggle to get started on a task, or forget to submit homework. He was resistant to seek help or ask questions in class for fear of getting reprimanded.

For years, his parents felt there was "something" getting in the way of his learning, but they couldn't put their fingers on it. Brendan's teachers reassured his parents he could do the work—he just needed to "try harder." Described as someone who could "turn it on when he wants to," this frustrated his parents and Brendan. Though they all agreed his grades didn't reflect his true ability, they were perplexed about why he had trouble applying himself consistently. Finally, he got tested and was diagnosed with ADHD, inattentive type.

With Brendan's senior year looming, he was concerned about his future. Although he didn't consider himself "college material," he wanted to attend college, was motivated to improve, and agreed to meet with me weekly.

Given what we've discussed, what might support Brendan?

After reviewing his testing, history, and work samples, our meetings included:

- identifying his strengths, inconsistencies, and challenges
- discussing his thoughts about "change" and how to use neuroplasticity to his advantage
- introducing systems for notetaking, homework, and meeting deadlines
- developing a growth mindset
- helping Brendan's teachers and parents understand EF, his strengths and needs, and ways to support him at school/home

By year's end, Brendan was empowered with strategies to learn efficiently. The change in his mindset and skill set was remarkable. In September of his senior year, he didn't see college as a realistic goal; by April, he was accepted to a competitive university. Four years later, he graduated with honors!

QUESTIONS to CONSIDER

1. How can you help the student(s) you identified earlier in this chapter develop healthier narratives about themselves as learners?

2. What school, home, and extra-curricular experiences helped or hindered the development of your EF? How does your neurodiversity affect your learning and life?

3. How would you rate the explicit instruction your students receive in EF to prepare them for success in school, relationships, jobs, and life? What needs changing?

4. Think of your students with neurodiversity and EF challenges. How do you typically respond to and explicitly support them? How do you view differently students who may have been misunderstood?

KEY POINTS

- Executive function involves self-driven, goal-directed behavior that guides future direction and utilizes the highest aspects of brain functions to organize, prioritize, and manage daily life.

- Students with underdeveloped EF often need SEL support.

- Emotions impact learning—for better or worse.

- Students with EF issues often experience high stress and academic challenges, which can lead to doubting themselves as learners and viewing school in a negative light.

- Students' brains continue to develop and change based on how they're used by a process called neuroplasticity.

- Genetics and environment affect executive function and neurodiversity.

2

Executive Dysfunction and Its Impact

If you go to work on your goals, your goals will go to work on you. If you go to work on your plan, it will go to work on you. Whatever good things we build end up building us.

Jim Rohn

Which of your students (past or present) stare blankly at a page or put their heads down on their desks when assigned a writing, reading, or math task? How about those who consistently arrive late, struggle with transitions, or fumble social interactions? Which ones wait until the last minute to complete assignments? If any of these behaviors resonate, you're not alone!

Whether you teach, support, or parent kids with executive dysfunction, it's important to know how it impacts their learning and quality of daily life. Research has found that executive function is not only a predictor of math and reading success, but it is "more important for school readiness than are IQ or entry-level reading or math."[17] In this chapter, we will identify common EF challenges with reading, writing, math, relationships, transitions, time management, homework, and notetaking, along with ways to help.

Impact on Reading

Reading takes hard work. To be successful readers, students must "juggle" various rules and strategies regarding letter sounds, spelling, decoding, word meanings, sentence structure, and comprehension, all while connecting information from long-term memory to new information. Kids

15-MINUTE FOCUS
Executive Function: Strategies to Build Underdeveloped Skills,
Maximize Learning, and Unlock Potential

must integrate and synchronize these skills while keeping themselves focused and self-regulated. A juggling act indeed!

Students who struggle with the five components of reading—phonemic awareness, phonics, fluency, vocabulary, and comprehension—may also be weak in EF. Even kids with stellar word recognition skills can surprise you; they may read beautifully out loud but not remember a lick of what they read. Recent research shows that EF helps students coordinate various reading components to comprehend text.[18] Imagine how daunting and anxiety-provoking reading must feel for students lagging in these areas.

Hollis Scarborough's updated visual of her Reading Rope (2012) reinforces the connection of EF to reading by weaving it around the various strands of word recognition and language comprehension components to form a strong rope.[19] For kids to become proficient readers, they need support with EF in addition to drill and practice with all these strands.

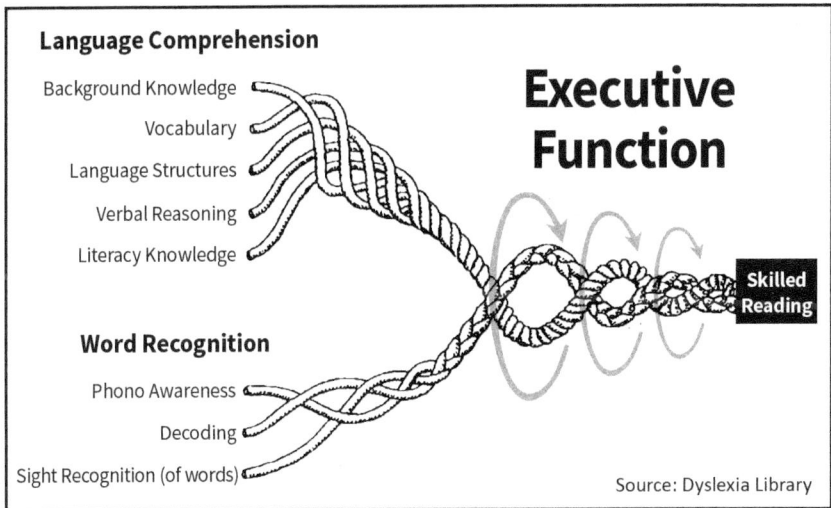

Language Comprehension
- Background Knowledge
- Vocabulary
- Language Structures
- Verbal Reasoning
- Literacy Knowledge

Executive Function

Skilled Reading

Word Recognition
- Phono Awareness
- Decoding
- Sight Recognition (of words)

Source: Dyslexia Library

Good readers tend to be highly active and engaged, applying a range of skills and strategies as they read, while kids with executive dysfunction tend to lack these skills. As students transition from "learning to read" to "reading to learn" by the end of third grade, they must extract key information, comprehend what they read, and increase their vocabulary. Lagging in these skills affects their ability to understand, discuss, analyze, gather information, or do homework assignments.

Reading skills are the collective responsibility of all educators and parents, as reading is critical to academic, career, and daily tasks. We must avoid "assumicide," thinking students have mastered certain reading and EF skills by a particular age or grade. You might be working with students who have advanced to a new grade yet lack some of the following skills:

How Executive Dysfunction Can Impact Reading[20]

GOAL SETTING	• Students might not know why they're reading or its purpose (i.e., quick facts, close reading).

PLANNING/ PRIORITIZING	• Students might not:
	  – use a calendar to schedule a "good" time/place to read (i.e., rested, fed, hydrated, away from distractions). Kids might want to read on their bed versus in a chair or at a table or desk.
	  – bring materials (book, notebook, pencil, highlighter, etc.)
	  – apply reading strategies (i.e., preview text, ask questions, analyze text structure)
	  – hone in on what's most important

ORGANIZATION	• Students may:
	  – lack systems for gathering, sequencing, categorizing, and managing information
	  – be unaware of commonalities and differences in text structures (i.e., narrative, informational, opinion/ argumentative)

TASK INITIATION	• Students may procrastinate, especially if don't like the topic or feel they're not good at reading.
TIME MANAGEMENT	• Students might not stick to deadlines, use a timer, schedule short breaks, estimate reading time, or break tasks into chunks.

15-MINUTE FOCUS
Executive Function: Strategies to Build Underdeveloped Skills,
Maximize Learning, and Unlock Potential

How Executive Dysfunction Can Impact Reading

WORKING MEMORY	• Students might have difficulty with:
	  – identifying subjects/verbs or main ideas/details, particularly in complex/compound sentences. (Lengthy sections will be harder to derive meaning and remember what's most important.)
	  – connecting new details with previous knowledge
	  – using text clues and strategies to generate main ideas/details or make inferences
	  – notetaking, organizing information, paraphrasing, or summarizing
	  – phonemic awareness (how sounds in words work)
	  – phonics (i.e., applying word patterns, syllable types, and word attack skills to new words; may be so focused on these skills, they lose meaning in what they read)
	  – fluency (i.e., pacing, intonation, paying attention to punctuation)
	  – vocabulary (might forget definitions or fail to use context clues)

FOCUS	• Students may:
	  – find it hard to sit quietly for a period and ignore distractions, especially with assigned readings or subjects not interesting to the student
	  – get lost in the details or focus on something interesting **to them** but miss key parts/points
	  – not notice text features/structures, essential and non-essential details or differences between similar looking words or letters
	  – not know what to do to stay alert (i.e., bring snack, movement break)
	  – not know how to color code or customize font size/words per page
	  – lack concentration to apply "rules" to all five reading components

EFFORT/MINDSET	• Students might lack consistent stamina, motivation, and productive talk about task and self as a reader

How Executive Dysfunction Can Impact Reading	

COGNITIVE FLEXIBILITY	• Students might:
	  – take things literally and have trouble with homonyms, words with multiple meanings (i.e., coast and bank), or atypical patterns
	  – find it hard to switch from different reading skills (i.e., decoding to comprehending) sections, or tasks (i.e., character traits to theme)
	  – miss context clues (i.e., pictures or certain words)
	  – not adjust behavior or strategies to meet reading goals

RESPONSE INHIBITION	• Students may find it hard to ignore irrelevant details/parts while reading; may daydream, blurt, or react, especially if the reading doesn't interest the student

SELF-REGULATION	• Students may:
	  – need help understanding the relevance behind the task and connection to the goal
	  – not maintain a good emotional state for learning, productivity, and feedback, especially if they didn't choose the text
	  – lack stress management or growth mindset strategies

SELF-MONITORING	• Students might:
	  – not ask for help, self-assess, or know or utilize strategies when they are confused
	  – continue with an unsuccessful plan
	  – work too fast without regard for accuracy or quality
	  – not know it's wise to slow down when reading new vocabulary, concepts, or complex sentences

Comprehension Support

While it is not within the scope of this book to specify interventions for each reading component, the following table lists skills that strengthen weak EF and comprehension. Teaching kids how texts are organized and how to access main ideas and supporting details can boost reading skills and academic performance. These, and other strategies mentioned throughout the book, help kids grow their focus, planning, prioritizing, memory, and self-monitoring muscles.

TEXT FEATURES	TEXT STRUCTURES	COMPREHENSION MONITORING
• Title • Table of Contents • Headings/ Subheadings • Captions • Index • Glossary	• Types of writing (informational, argumentative, narrative) • Genres (biography, poem, fable, etc.) • Introduction and conclusion • Transitional words • Patterns of organization (i.e., description, sequence, problem/solution, cause/effect, compare/ contrast)	• Categorizing • Stated main ideas • Inferred main ideas • Graphic organizers • Notetaking • Question generating • Summarizing

Source: Keys to Literacy

Impact on Writing

Like reading, writing is a complex task necessary for school and career success. Unlike reading, which begins with words already on the page, writing starts with a blank page and requires students to cue, coordinate, and produce their thoughts on paper in an organized fashion, often on demand. Writing is a way to communicate ideas by "thinking on paper."[21] Students must use EF throughout the process to juggle decisions about topic, audience, task, purpose, word use, style, sentence structure, supporting details, conventions, and handwriting, all while keeping their emotions in check. Yep, more juggling!

Like the transition from "learning to read" to "reading to learn," kids must segue from "learning to write" to "writing to learn," which requires the integration of text generation (generating ideas), transcription (putting ideas to paper), and EF.[22] Students who are weak in working memory might find it challenging to write essays, create reports, and answer questions on tests and homework. They may devote a lot of energy to remember handwriting or spelling rules and be left with little stamina to generate their ideas and get them on paper, like kids who put great effort into decoding and run out of steam to make meaning of the text.

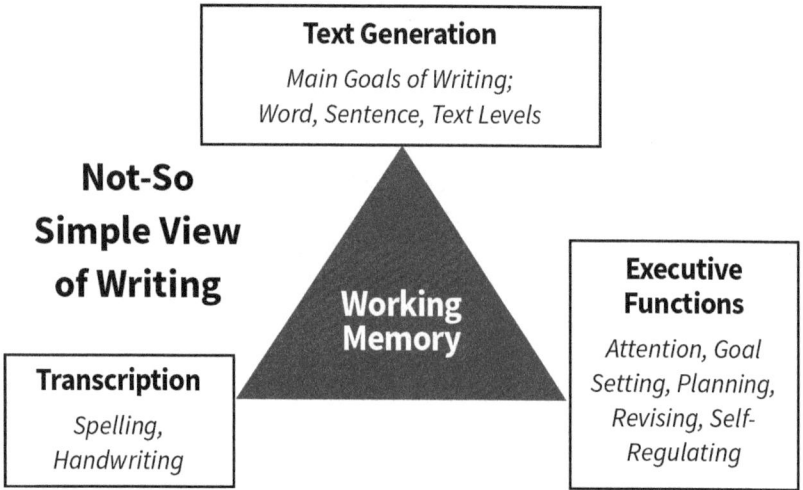

Not-So Simple View of Writing

Text Generation
*Main Goals of Writing;
Word, Sentence, Text Levels*

Working Memory

Executive Functions
Attention, Goal Setting, Planning, Revising, Self-Regulating

Transcription
Spelling, Handwriting

Source: Keys to Literacy

When you consider how essential writing is to school success, it's no surprise that kids with EF gaps may feel anxious, frustrated, or overwhelmed when it comes time to write. They may have experienced previous failures with writing, feel embarrassed about their deficits, or fear making a mistake. They might avoid writing tasks, have a meltdown, or not know how to begin, especially when doing open-ended or long-term assignments. They may lack a mental blueprint of the finished product, which can trigger negative self-talk (i.e., "I'm not good at writing" or "I'm stuck. I may as well quit"). If students don't have a plan to approach writing or lack productive self-talk to push through setbacks or negative thoughts, they can quickly unravel, demonstrate learned helplessness, or give up before even starting. Like reading, good writers tend to actively apply a range of skills and strategies throughout the process, but that's not often the case with students who experience executive dysfunction.

How Executive Dysfunction Can Impact Writing

GOAL SETTING	• Students may need help setting a purpose (i.e., persuade, contrast, inform).

PLANNING/ PRIORITIZING	• Students might not:
	  – use a calendar to set a good time to write (i.e., fed, rested, hydrated)
	  – choose a good place to write (i.e., sitting at a table or in a room without distractions)
	  – follow a writing process
	  – identify the task, audience, and purpose
	  – be aware that an audience can be real or imagined
	  – bring paper, pencil, or other essential supplies
	  – gather information with notes or graphic organizer
	  – translate ideas into sentences and paragraphs (dictating their thoughts to someone may help)
	  – revise and proofread for conventions
	  – generate a final draft

ORGANIZATION	• Students might:
	  – have good ideas but not know how to organize them
	  – lack systems for gathering, ordering, sequencing, categorizing, and managing ideas and information
	  – be unaware of sentence/paragraph types and cues related to types of writing
	  – be unable to break up tasks into achievable steps, especially with long-term assignments

TASK INITIATION	• Students might:
	  – procrastinate, especially if they don't consider themselves writers
	  – not initiate stress-reducing strategies

TIME MANAGEMENT	• Students might:
	  – not use a calendar or planner to record tasks and deadlines, especially for long-term assignments
	  – under or over-estimate the time needed for writing tasks (i.e., they may complete a rough draft and think they're done)

How Executive Dysfunction Can Impact Writing

WORKING MEMORY	• Students might not remember:
	  – what they want to say and how to say it
	  – to use a writing process
	  – to sequence multiple steps or parts
	  – main ideas need supporting details
	  – rules for handwriting, typing, spelling, and conventions

FOCUS	• Students may have trouble zeroing in on each part of the writing process or sustaining concentration to stick with the task.

EFFORT/MINDSET	• Students might:
	  – find it difficult to maintain motivation and stamina
	  – need visible samples of productive self-talk about the task and themselves, especially if they don't see themselves as writers

COGNITIVE FLEXIBILITY	• Students may:
	  – find it hard to switch from different parts of the writing process (i.e., drafting to revising) or between sections/tasks
	  – not know how to adjust behavior or strategies to meet writing goals

RESPONSE INHIBITION	• Students may:
	  – have difficulty ignoring irrelevant details or parts that are interesting but not necessarily important
	  – daydream, blurt, or react, especially if they don't enjoy writing or didn't choose the topic

SELF-REGULATION	• Students might quickly unravel, not know productive self-talk, or not know how to keep emotions in check to receive feedback, especially if the task lacks relevance, they don't see themselves as a writer, or they didn't choose the topic.

How Executive Dysfunction Can Impact Writing	
SELF-MONITORING	• Students might:
	– not review their work to see if they followed directions or answered all parts of the question(s)
	– keep going if the assignment not going well, or if they think their work is done when the last word is written
	– not know what to proofread (i.e., tense switches, fragments, spelling, punctuation)

Writing Support

To flex kids' "writing muscles" and build stamina, they need daily opportunities to write in ALL content areas for a variety of purposes and lengths. Teaching kids about main ideas, text features, and sentence/text structures in reading also pays dividends in writing. When they understand how different kinds of texts and genres are built, they are better equipped to construct their own written pieces. Kids benefit from visual cues, explicit instruction, guided practice, and scaffolding with the subskills of writing. This includes a writing process to help them focus, organize, plan, and prioritize their ideas. Consider visuals such as:

The Writing Process

Think & Plan	
Write	
Revise	

Source: Keys to Literacy

The Hamburger Paragraph

Topic Sentence
Juicy Details #1
Juicy Details #2
Juicy Details #3
Closing Sentence

Source: Inspired Elementary Literacy in Focus

Impact on Math

The link between executive function also affects math comprehension and skills development. Math tasks require students to use and build on their previous knowledge and shift back and forth between information or parts to complete a problem. This requires them to alternate between their analytical skills and working memory. When doing word problems, kids must use their reading skills as they keep numbers, steps, rules, and questions in mind to figure out which approach works best.[23] Those with weak working memory might have trouble retaining needed information or remember how to apply it. Unsurprisingly, students who haven't mastered basic math facts but are expected to apply them in math problems will find these tasks frustrating.

For math-phobic kids, anxiety can interfere with their ability to complete an assignment. They may freeze when it is time to start a math task or be stuck in their worries instead of listening to the directions. After you explain the steps, they might ask, "What are we doing?" Alternately, they may dive in without reading the directions closely. Your students' behavior can stem from a lack of proficiency with math, EF, metacognitive self-talk, productive responses to stress/anxiety, or all of the above.

The **How Executive Dysfunction Can Impact Math Chart** and the following graphic reinforce the link between math and executive function:

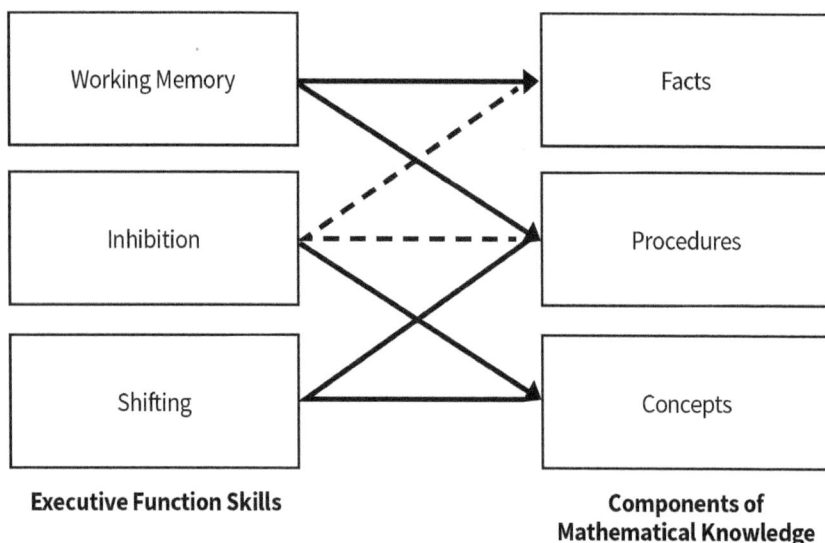

Executive Function Skills

Components of Mathematical Knowledge

Source: Science Direct

How Executive Dysfunction Can Impact Math

GOAL SETTING	• Kids might set a goal that's too high or low (or not set one at all).
PLANNING/ PRIORITIZING	• Students may miss parts of directions and not underline key words or look over a problem/assignment.

ORGANIZATION	• Students might:
	  – be unaware of rules, steps, and relationships (i.e., sorting)
	  – randomly scribble problems across their paper instead of lining them up

TASK INITIATION	• Students may avoid starting work if anxious or don't think they are good at math.

TIME MANAGEMENT	• Students might not:
	  – schedule when to do work and predict how long it takes
	  – use a timer or pace themselves (i.e., work too fast or spend too much time on one problem)

WORKING MEMORY	• Students may:
	  – find it hard to memorize math facts, do "mental math," apply previous knowledge, and retain directions, steps, or formulas to complete problems in the proper sequence
	  – forget one part of a problem while working on another part

FOCUS	• Students may find it hard to:
	  – focus while teacher explains concepts, terms, or directions
	  – stay on task, revisit directions, and maintain concentration
	  – pay attention to signs and steps (i.e., adding instead of subtracting)

EFFORT/MINDSET	• Students may lack motivation or productive talk about the task and themselves, especially if they don't think they are good at math.

How Executive Dysfunction Can Impact Math	

COGNITIVE FLEXIBILITY	• Students may find it difficult to:
	  – apply rules from previous math knowledge to new problems
	  – adjust behavior or approach, thinking there is only "one" way
	  – switch from one step/procedure to another (i.e., adding to multiplying)

RESPONSE INHIBITION	• Students might find it hard to:
	  – ignore irrelevant details of a word problem
	  – filter out incorrect answers related to numbers (i.e., three is bigger than two, but not as a denominator in fractions such as 1/3 and ½)
	  – resist temptation to rush, daydream, or blurt out the first answer that comes to mind (i.e., if reviewing 5+5=10, a kid might say 5-5=10)[24]

SELF-REGULATION	• Students may find it difficult to manage stress and maintain a good emotional state for learning, productivity, and feedback.
SELF-MONITORING	• Students might not evaluate if answers make sense or use a personalized "checklist" to catch and correct errors.

Impact on Relationships

Healthy interactions play a significant role in the development of EF and SEL, starting in the first years of life. Research shows that kids lacking positive connections with their teachers often show a decrease in their task initiation, social skills, and frustration tolerance while their behavioral problems increase, especially for boys.[25]

Kids with EF challenges may present as spontaneous, creative, and energetic. On the flip side, they may be prone to impulsivity, unreliability, argumentativeness, and tantrums. As students get older, poor impulse control can lead to partaking in risky behaviors with driving, alcohol, and drug use.

The following chart addresses other common ways EF issues can affect relationships:

How Executive Dysfunction Can Impact Relationships

GOAL SETTING	• Students often remain in the "here and now" and are less likely to prepare for the future and set goals.
PLANNING/ PRIORITIZING	• Students might need help breaking the day/week/tasks into chunks and prioritizing what comes first.
ORGANIZATION	• Students might: – not put things away after use or keep space neat – be "all over the place" with thoughts and ideas when talking – lack systems to keep track of commitments, information, items, etc.
TASK INITIATION	• Students might: – wait to act until last minute or things become urgent – not start chores/tasks without reminders or finish within expected time frames/deadlines
TIME MANAGEMENT	• Students may: – be unaware of consequences of being late for assignments, obligations, appointments, etc. – over or underestimate how long tasks take or fail to complete tasks in timely fashion
WORKING MEMORY	• Students might not remember: – important dates, meetings, or what needs to be done – strategies and when to use them
FOCUS	• Students might: – be distracted or hyper-focused on something of interest and miss what is being said (i.e., dinner time, time to go) – find it hard to sit still, look at person talking, and not be distracted by who or what's around them (i.e., devices); may be unable to resume work if interrupted. – miss cues or "read the room" (i.e., may make a loud entrance while others are reading quietly)

How Executive Dysfunction Can Impact Relationships	
EFFORT/MINDSET	• Students may lack positive self-talk or have trouble staying motivated to improve and implement feedback.

COGNITIVE FLEXIBILITY	• Students may find it hard to:
	  – transition from something they like to something they dislike
	  – see someone else's perspective or "go with the flow" when plans change

RESPONSE INHIBITION	• Students may:
	  – be prone to "cross the line" and not think before responding
	  – interrupt, get bored easily, or have difficulty taking turns, sharing toys, or waiting
	  – have trouble stopping an enjoyable activity (i.e., a game or book) or leaving a place they enjoy (i.e., the playground or a friend's house)

SELF-REGULATION	• Students may:
	  – be prone to tantrums, overreact to something seemingly trivial, or underreact to urgent matters
	  – appear defensive to feedback

SELF-MONITORING	• Students may not learn easily from past mistakes, make changes in their behavior, or notice when off-track or being self-consumed.

Impact on Time

Students with executive dysfunction can experience "time blindness"[26] and have difficulty with time estimation, passage, pacing, and management. They may think in open-ended terms, focus on the present versus the future, and not "feel" the urgency to nail down a time to start a task or record deadlines in a calendar or planner.

The **Time Thieves Worksheet** and following activities integrate cues and strategies to develop time-building skills:

NAME: _____   DATE: _____

Time Thieves

Check any "thieves" that apply. Then, problem-solve how to address each.

		Problem-Solving Ideas
MY BODY	❏ Tired ❏ Hungry ❏ Thirsty ❏ Muscle tightness, fast heartbeat, headache, etc. Other: _____	
MY APPROACH	❏ I'm unclear about the goal or "finished product." ❏ I lack a plan. ❏ I tend to procrastinate. ❏ I want everything to be perfect. Other: _____	
MY ORGANIZATION	❏ I often come unprepared. (i.e. directions, pen, book, etc.) ❏ I have trouble remembering or finding what I need. ❏ I don't know how or where to start. ❏ I don't have a system for organizing my ideas, belongings, etc. Other: _____	
MY LOCATION	❏ Social distractions ❏ Frequent interruptions ❏ Too noisy Other: _____	
MY DIGITAL DISTRACTIONS	❏ Phone ❏ Computer ❏ Social media ❏ Video games ❏ YouTube videos Other: _____	
MY EMOTIONS	I need to learn how to manage: ❏ Anger ❏ Frustration ❏ Anxiety ❏ Boredom ❏ Lack of Relevance to what I'm doing Other: _____	
OTHER	❏ _____ ❏ _____ ❏ _____	

15-Minute Focus: Executive Function: Strategies to Build Underdeveloped Skills, Maximize Learning, and Unlock Potential by Noël Foy
© National Center for Youth Issues · www.ncyi.org

Analog Clock

Compared to a digital version, an analog clock helps kids see the incremental passage of time. When using this kind of clock, you can ask students to:

- Estimate how long a task might take to complete. This can be abstract for kids, so have them think of something concrete they're familiar with (i.e., brush teeth, feed fish).
- shade in a segment needed for the task, and mark a check-in point (i.e., halfway through it)
- jot down start and end times. Once the project is done, you can ask, "Did it take more or less time than expected? If Time Thieves got in the way, what can you do differently?"

Pomodoro Technique

I find this process particularly helpful for kids who procrastinate. Here's how it works:

1. Turn off all distractions (put digital devices in another room).
2. Set a timer for 25 minutes.
3. Focus on the task at hand. It's okay to jot down on a sticky note something that comes to mind (i.e., remember to walk the dog, text a specific friend), but get right back to the work.
4. When the timer sounds, reward yourself (or the child) with a 5-minute break.

It's effective because:

- it gives the brain practice with bursts of focused attention (a 25-minute duration seems doable)
- short breaks clear the mind for new learning. Breaks give the brain a rest from focusing so it can encode new information and skills into long-term memory.
- the brain starts to focus on the process, not the outcome
- anticipation of a reward helps with motivation.[27] Once students see evidence of progress, it is easier to keep going.

Planning Tools

Schedules, calendars, and planners can be utilized to keep important information and cue students to what comes next, how their day will unfold, and how they'll schedule their time, especially if they have multiple commitments on the same day (i.e., assignments, meetings, or activities). Post these "holding" tools in prominent spots to build cognitive flexibility, provide a mental picture of how the day is chunked, and when to do each activity. This takes stress off the brain and decreases the chance of missing something important. It also prevents wasted time and frustration, freeing kids up to do more of what interests them!

Teachers often remind their students to use planning tools, but they may not know *how* to use them. As with any other skill, kids benefit from explicit instruction and guided practice. When you assign work and deadlines, demonstrate what this looks like, thinking aloud as you use your calendar, planner, sticky notes, alarms, or reminder notifications. Experiment with whether digital or paper options work best for your students, and ask them to bring their calendar/planner with them. (You will want back-up online versions). Make these practices part of your routine to boost kids' time management, organization, focus, task initiation, planning/prioritizing, and self-regulation.[28]

Long-Term Assignments

Long-term assignments can be a real bugaboo for kids with EF challenges. With so much information to juggle, they benefit from seeing a sample of a "finished product," thinking through all parts or steps of an assignment, and breaking parts into chunks with assigned deadlines. Some students might not realize they have to read a chapter (or an entire book) first before starting a writing assignment, so have students record the assignment's final due date and then work backwards, setting deadlines for each task (i.e., final essay, revised draft, first draft, research, outline, topic choice).

Make Planning Visible

This visual system from Sarah Ward and Kristen Jacobsen, co-authors and creators of the 360 Thinking Program,[29] is particularly helpful for managing long-term assignments.

1. Students choose a colored sticky note strip and write down on the strip **one** specific responsibility to do for a subject or project with time estimate (i.e., take notes for 30 minutes).
2. On a calendar or planner, students place the strip on the day they plan to do the work. If the planner has time slots, place strip(s) in the desired slot(s).
3. After completing each responsibility, students throw away the strip. If they don't complete the task on the day planned, they move the strip to the next day, making the planning tangible. Kids see their progression and how tasks can pile up if not completed (i.e., 10-20 minutes not spent on today's task adds more work tomorrow).

Depending on the number of steps to an assignment, students might have a strip on their planner for each day of the week or just certain days. If students have other long-term tasks (i.e., test or project) due around the same time, color code the sticky notes to represent each task, and repeat the above three steps.

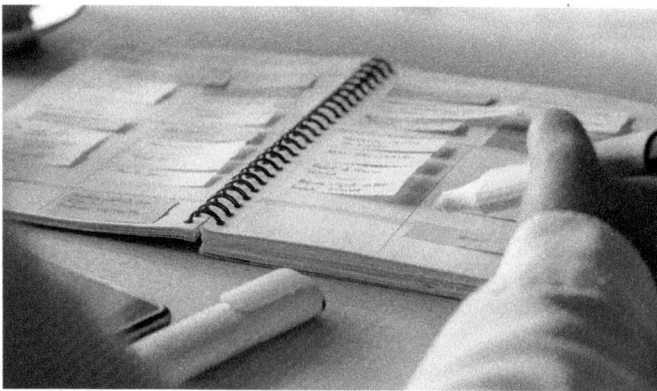

Impact on Transitions

You've probably asked your students to come in from recess or put away materials for one class before starting another. At home, you might have asked your kids to stop playing video games and begin their homework. What seem like simple transitions can be difficult for neurodiverse learners and kids with executive dysfunction and/or anxiety. It can be hard to stop what they are in the middle of, especially if it's interesting or enjoyable. Context matters!

Transitions are common in school, work, and life, requiring the application of cognitive flexibility, planning, and response inhibition. However, many students with EF challenges are expected to make transitions without receiving much support. Often, kids don't have a clear picture in their mind of the next task or activity. Behavior Analyst Jessica Minahan reminds us, "Students need to make a mental shift before a physical one."[30] For instance, if transitioning from physical education (PE) class to science, students must stop focusing on PE and begin thinking about science expectations (i.e., sitting at their desk with a notebook or doing a lab).

How can you help transitions go smoother? Try Minahan's suggestions:[31]

Part 1: Give a good stopping or end point.

Say, "Stop at the bottom of page five" or "Three more jumps on the trampoline, and it's time to go." If you're stopping an activity that is not finished, say, "pause" instead of "stop." Help kids imagine "pressing the pause button" on a remote; it sends a different message to the brain than a "hard stop."

Part 2: Help students make a mental picture of the next activity.

Show a picture, video, or visual of students doing the next activity. If you can include you and your actual students in pictures or videos, even better!

Part 3: Mention when the next activity will start.

Try something like, "We're going to finish up math work and start story time in five minutes."

Part 4: Plan in advance if there is waiting time.

Kids with EF issues likely need to learn the skill of waiting, and they need clarity about what they can or cannot do while waiting. If you are circulating the room to help students, provide cognitive distractions (i.e., crossword puzzle, doodle pad) or quick tasks (i.e., stacking chairs, collecting papers) for other kids to do while waiting. Avoid offering activities that are too enjoyable; those can be harder to stop midstream.

For students who find transitions especially difficult, try an "in between step." For example, if transitioning from recess to math, consider a brief meditation, math video, or drawing activity. With students already seated (possibly using a pencil and paper), the transition is a bit easier.

Impact on Homework

Homework woes can be especially problematic and stressful for kids with executive dysfunction. It helps to start homework around the same time each day instead of waiting for kids to feel inspired, which probably won't happen until panic sets in at 10 p.m.!

For better results, try these tips:

- Choose an effective workspace with materials handy.
- Address Time Thieves. Are noise-canceling headphones or a trifold board needed to reduce distractions?
- Do the Pomodoro Technique (with a timer), especially for procrastinators.
- Have students return assignments directly into their backpacks upon completion.
- Use a Homework Log that reinforces EF, as shown in the following example, slightly modified from Landmark School:[32]

NAME: _____ DATE: _____

Homework Log (Example)

CLASS/ASSIGNMENT	TIME PREDICTION	START TIME	END TIME	LOCATION	TIME THIEVES	FIXED OR GROWTH MINDSET
ELA–write opinion paragraph	30 min.	4:00	4:45	Kitchen Table	Forgot sheet	Fixed
Math sheet, odd numbers	15 min	5:00	5:30	Kitchen Table	Distracted by people	Both
Social Studies–read pgs 30-33 w/ 3 takeaways	10 min	7:00	7:20	Desk in my room	Phone	Growth
Biology–finish lab conclusion	15 min.	7:30	8:00	Bed	Felt tired	Both
French–study vocab	15 min.	8:15	8:30	Bed	More tired	Fixed

Note: You will find information about mindset in Chapter 3 and additional strategies to address homework issues in Chapter 5.

I'll never get this math...I give up!

Mmmm...I forget the steps to the assignment.

Should I start homework or check my phone?

I wonder how long the reading will take...

I don't know where to start!

Should I work in my room or the kitchen?

Impact on Notetaking

Notetaking is a valuable skill in school and beyond. Kids with organization, planning, and prioritizing challenges might take disorganized notes lacking key information (if they take notes at all!). Here are some ways to help:[33]

- **Cognitive Flexibility:** Figure out which notetaking format options work best for students (i.e., two-column notes, outline). Some prefer writing their notes by hand, while others gravitate to a digital system.
- **Focus:** Notice verbal/written cues that signal something is significant (i.e., text features, images, color coding, underlined/boxed sections, or key phrases such as, "Three factors that led to…," or "The most important reason…").
- **Organize Approach:** Narratives can be organized around story structure (setting, characters, events, etc.) or by beginning, middle, and end. Informational text can be organized by topics/sub-topics and main ideas/details.
- **Time Savers:** Instead of writing complete sentences, teach kids how to paraphrase, abbreviate, and use visual cues (i.e., arrows, parentheses).

Kids might need guidance developing a notebook system to file important handouts and write notes in specific sections for each class instead of using random pages. Notebooks with inside folders or pockets work well for some kids, while others prefer binders with subject dividers and a three-hole punch or a separate accordion folder to keep important papers from disappearing. Moreover, students will likely need a system for keeping their backpacks in order.

Foundational Strategies

In addition to the skill-building suggestions discussed so far, the general strategies below boost content knowledge, skills, and EF for anything "read, said, or done"[34] and lay the foundation for many of the specific strategies to follow in the upcoming chapters:

- **Metacognitive Awareness**: Help kids understand how they learn and approach tasks.
- **Echo Response:** Say directions, terms, etc. out loud and have kids repeat them back. You can pair this with movement—act out vocabulary, steps, or concepts (i.e., rise over run).
- **Connecting to Prior Knowledge**: Help kids see relationships between background knowledge and new information (i.e., graphic organizers).

- **Organizing Strategies:** Teach kids how to organize and gather information (i.e., graphic organizers, templates, notetaking systems).
- **Predicting:** Notice written or verbal clues.
- **Visualizing**: Use graphic organizers, images, charts, and drawings.
- **Collaborative Problem-Solving**: Discuss different approaches/ways of thinking (i.e., have kids make up math problems, swap with a partner, and share answers).
- **Self-Questioning**: Generate questions along Bloom's Taxonomy continuum before, during, and after reading or learning. Questions can be answered individually, with a partner, or group.

Blooms Taxonomy

Create	Use Existing Information to Make Something New *Invent, Develop, Design, Compose, Generate, Construct*
Evaluate	Make Judgments Based on Sound Analysis *Assess, Judge, Defend, Prioritize, Critique, Recommend*
Analyze	Explore Relationships, Causes, and Connections *Compare, Contrast, Categorize, Organize, Distinguish*
Apply	Use Existing Knowledge in New Contexts *Practice, Calculate, Implement, Operate, Use, Illustrate*
Understand	Grasp the Meaning of Something *Explain, Paraphrase, Report, Describe, Summarize*
Remember	Retain and Recall Information *Reiterate, Memorize, Duplicate, Repeat, Identify*

Source: Helpful Professor

Reduce Cognitive Overload

As students learn new content and skills, they may over-tax their working memory and attempt to process too much information, leaving them overwhelmed, exhausted, forgetful, or anxious. This affects learning, focus, behavior, mood, and productivity. Academics, relationships, time management, transitions, and homework place high cognitive demands on kids with executive dysfunction. To reduce cognitive overload and increase EF, integrate the following tips:[35]

- Give explicit, step-by-step directions; have students repeat back to you and provide a written copy of the steps.
- Underline/highlight key words or parts of directions.
- State or show just one direction, step, or part at a time.
- Partially complete a bit of the work (i.e., providing a topic sentence or the first step to a math problem).
- Make tasks close-ended and provide scaffolds (i.e., sentence starters, word banks, templates, models of finished work).
- Break assignments/problems into chunks.
- Use mnemonics.
- Make personalized checklists of things to "look out for."
- Take short breaks.
- Offer the choice of work being done in written, verbal, or graphic form (reduce length if needed).
- Provide text-to-speech tools or other technological supports.
- Give effective feedback.
- Provide ample "think and wait time" after asking questions.

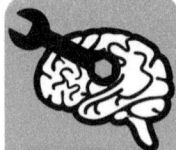

First Thirty Seconds

I find this tip a game changer: the first thirty seconds of an activity or task are the most important, especially for students who have anxiety or difficulty getting started. These students benefit from having a sentence frame to start writing or the first problem on a math sheet completed. You don't want kids sitting at their desks ruminating on how they despise a task, as they can quickly become distracted, reactive and shut down. As you leave the student, say something like, "I can't wait to see what you do with this!"[36]

Student Story

Niles, a second-grade student with stellar decoding, syllabicating, and fluency, enjoyed reading out loud in front of the class. However, when asked to retell or summarize a story, he'd respond in a disorganized fashion, draw inaccurate conclusions, or miss key events and characters.

Even though Niles didn't present as a struggling reader, he struggled with comprehension, as he derived little meaning from what he read. Testing revealed EF challenges, especially low working memory. No wonder he had difficulty "holding on" to essential details, characters, and events.

Difficulties with attention, focus, and working memory were also apparent when given multi-step directions, especially for writing tasks and transitions. Niles would space out or show signs of fatigue, often putting his head down on the desk. When his teacher asked why he hadn't started, he'd say, "I don't know what to do." He'd also get antsy during transitions and talk to peers or wander around the room when he was supposed to line up or listen to the teacher. After directions were given, he'd frequently ask, "What are we doing?"

Given what we've discussed, what might support Niles?

My work with Niles centered on strategies to decrease stress and cognitive overload and boost his focus, attention, working memory, comprehension, and writing skills. I supported his teachers, school counselor, and parents with information about EF and how it affected Niles.

Before long, Niles applied comprehension strategies to his reading assignments. When given a sentence frame, he was able to start writing tasks. He developed better self-awareness and lowered his stress by doing regular Mind/Body Checks and 4/6 breathing (Chapter 3). A strategy called Match the Picture (Chapter 5) helped him internalize his morning, after school, and homework routines. Niles used these strategies at home, school, and extracurriculars, resulting in more confidence, efficiency, and autonomy.

QUESTIONS to CONSIDER

1. Using information from this chapter, which gaps do you notice in your students?
- reading
- writing
- math
- relationship
- time management
- transition
- notetaking skills

2. How do you envision providing more explicit instruction and guided practice to address these gaps?

3. What can you see yourself integrating to help your students?
- get started on tasks
- manage long-term assignments
- boost homework efficiency
- decrease cognitive overload

KEY POINTS

- Executive dysfunction can impact students' reading, writing, math, relationships, time management, homework, notetaking, and transitions.

- "Good" readers and writers tend to be highly active and engaged during the process, while kids with EF challenges often lack strategies in these areas.

- Students with executive dysfunction benefit from structure, explicit instruction, guided practice, and scaffolding.

- Anxiety, a lack of metacognitive self-talk, and underdeveloped proficiency with a skill or subject can increase student reluctance.

- Cognitive overload affects learning, focus, behavior, mood, and productivity.

3

When Stress Goes Up, Learning Goes Down

We feel, therefore, we learn.

Mary Helen Immordino-Yang

To fully understand executive function, stress needs to be part of the conversation. Learning about the impact of stress was a "lightbulb moment" for me, sparking productive changes in my approaches to teaching, coaching, and parenting. This knowledge helped me understand why I froze in my high school science class and didn't remember a lick of what the teacher said. Moreover, I had a new lens from which to view the behaviors I was observing in schools. Perhaps kids who acted out, spaced out, or seemed stuck weren't doing so because they *wanted* to, but because the stress response was doing its job.

It seems so obvious now, but it wasn't until relatively late in life that I fully appreciated the connection between emotion and learning. I learned that the brain experiences stress as:

- anxiety
- frustration
- anger
- boredom
- lack of relevance to what you are learning or doing

When students—of any learning profile—are in immersed in these emotions, they're not receptive to learning.[37]

As an anxious child who frequently worried about taking tests, raising my hand in class, or performing in recitals, I didn't know what to do when anxiety struck. Worry bossed me around and told me I couldn't handle or do certain things. I had no idea I could talk back to it, reframe my thoughts, and reset my body and mind. I didn't know about the impact of anxiety on my ability to learn, remember information, think critically, and perform.

I want to give hope to kids who feel the same way I did. While we can't eradicate anxiety, we can learn how to manage it. When anxiety shows up in your environment, *and it will*, you need to know what to do and say, especially since about 30% of kids exhibit symptoms of an anxiety disorder.[38] Though there is no one-size-fits-all remedy, this chapter provides quick, real-time solutions to reduce stress, better meet students' social, emotional, and academic needs, and boost their learning, engagement, and motivation. Kids and adults need a toolbox of coping skills to self-regulate and juggle life's demands so that EF, behavior, and productivity don't suffer. Let's fill that toolbox!

Quick Mind/Body Check with 4/6 Breathing

I start my workshops, meetings, or classes with a quick mind/body check. It's an opportunity to build self-awareness, meet my student(s) or audience "where they are," and get them ready to learn. This exercise only takes a few minutes and can be done anytime, anyplace. It allows kids and adults to "check in so they don't check out," and notice their warning signs (i.e., distressing thoughts, how they are holding stress in their body). When paired with 4/6 breathing (my "go to"), a mind/body check can help increase focus and regulate the nervous system.

Mind/Body Check

I feel great!	I am feeling good.	I am feeling okay.	I am starting to struggle today.	I need to reach out for support today.

Source: Noel Foy, Neuro Noel Consulting (c). 2024.

If you notice kids starting to unravel, pause and say, "Let's do a mind/body check," and guide them through the following script. As kids become proficient at noticing their warning signs, they can apply this process independently. (Feel free to create your own script using visuals of your choice.)

> ## Mind/Body Check Sample with a 4/6 Breathing Script
>
> *Take a moment to notice the thoughts going on in our mind. Maybe you feel calm and comfortable, or perhaps you feel tired, anxious, or overwhelmed.*
>
> *Shift your focus to your body. Notice any tightness or tingling or other sensations, such as a fast heartbeat or a headache.*
>
> *Choose a category on the Mind/Body Check that's most "like you" in this moment. There's no right or wrong answer. [Students may share which category resonates, but it's not necessary.]*
>
> *If something in your mind or body might get in the way of your ability to learn, focus, or produce, it can help to shift your thoughts to your senses and regulate your nervous system with slow, deep breathing.*
>
> *Let's try what's called 4/6 breathing. Place one hand on your chest and one hand on your belly. Inhale for four seconds. Notice your chest and belly rise. Exhale for six seconds. Notice your chest and belly fall. [Repeat two more times.]*

Cultivate Low-Threat, High-Learning Environments

In Chapter 1, we talked about the importance of environment and its role in shaping healthy brains. The brain likes to learn in a calm, focused, and alert state to take in new information, connect it to what it has previously learned, and use it for later retrieval. It responds well to a low-threat, welcoming environment in which individuals feel valued, heard, and respected. Kindness, enthusiasm, and connection go a long way in lowering stress, promoting academic risk-taking, and developing a sense of trust, respect, curiosity, and community.

Because emotion and learning are interconnected, an environment with healthy interpersonal connections drives learning, boosts engagement, and releases oxytocin—a happy brain chemical that contributes to keeping students' EF online.[39] When learning takes place in safe, inspiring, and empowering environments, you have an awesome opportunity to enhance the powerful connection of emotion to learning while shaping students' brains in optimal ways.

Here are some ways to promote a "low stress, high learning" environment:

- Smile and greet your students by name.
- Use a daily mind/body check with 4/6 breathing at beginning of class or when needed.
- Verbally share details about schedules, routines, and expectations (including consequences), and provide written copies.
- Engage in two-minute chats to build relationships. Get to know kids and their interests on the way to/from class, at snack, etc.[40]
- Let kids know you care and believe in *all* of them (not just the "easy" ones).[41]
- Make mistakes a normal part of learning. Use positive, encouraging language to guide and correct rather than using shame and blame. Share your struggles, recognize academic risks, and have some fun while learning!
- Welcome feedback (brief, direct, and non-judgmental).
- Keep emotion out of the task and stick with the facts.

Teach Kids About the Stress Response

Kids need to know what's going on in their brain and body when they feel anxious, frustrated, angry, bored, or don't see relevance to what they're learning. A quick snow globe demonstration appeals to all ages and is a concrete way to introduce students to the stress response and how the brain does/does not like to learn. (A "glitter bottle" works well too.)

Clear Brain

Cloudy Brain

Clear/Cloudy Brain Demonstration and Script

Imagine this snow globe represents your brain, and the glitter at the bottom represents your thoughts, feelings, and all you've learned. We can see through the snow globe right now. It's clear and calm, which is how your brain likes to learn.

Watch what happens when you get angry, frustrated, anxious, or bored. This stresses the brain. [Shake the snow globe or have a student do so. Ask students to describe what they notice.] The swirly glitter represents how your thoughts and feelings get mixed up. When your brain is "cloudy," it's hard to remember what you've learned, because the "emotional brain" hijacks the "thinking brain."

Now, watch what happens when you "reset" yourself with 4/6 breathing [inhale for 4 seconds, exhale for 6 seconds]. Notice the glitter starts to settle to the bottom. The snow globe—and your brain—gradually becomes clear again. Now, with the "thinking brain" back in charge, you can learn, focus, and perform, whether you're doing math facts, playing the guitar, or kicking a soccer ball.

[Feel free to add details relevant to your student(s).]

How the Stress Response Works

With the snow globe introduction in mind, I want to share more details about how the stress response works, providing a visual to reference. I don't shy away from using sophisticated terms such as the pre-frontal cortex or amygdala. I believe kids can handle this vocabulary, especially if they hear you use it regularly. When you introduce the terms, say them out loud and have students repeat them back to you.

The Stress Response

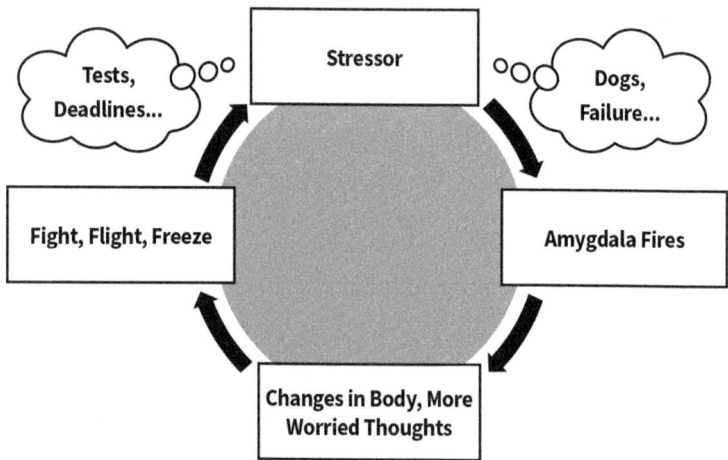

Source: Noel Foy, Neuro Noel Consulting (c). 2024

The following downloadable script is geared for grades 3 and up. (Feel free to use kid-friendly language to help with understanding the concepts but don't alter the scientific terms.)

The Stress Response Script

Worry begins in a part of your brain called the pre-frontal cortex. You might worry about taking tests, reading in front of the class, trying out for a team, or making friends.

[You/students can add other worries, if desired.]

Worry activates a part of your brain called the amygdala, which wants to protect you from danger. It releases stress chemicals in your body. You may notice muscle tightness, sweating, a rapid heartbeat, stomachache, or headache. Before you know it, you can experience what's called the fight, flight, or freeze response. You may find yourself acting out, zoning out, or feeling stuck. When this happens, your executive function (what you need to think, manage emotions, and get things done) goes offline, making it hard to remember information, behave your best, or start a task.

While your stress response is designed to protect you, it sometimes overreacts, just like a false alarm from the smoke detector in your home. Has burnt toast or old batteries ever set off the alarm in your house? That's similar to what happens in your brain when you worry. It might interpret situations as emergencies, such as forgetting the steps to a math problem or not knowing how to start a writing task. Your brain doesn't know the difference between real or imagined threats, so you might experience "false alarms," because the stress response is trying to protect you from something your brain thinks is dangerous.[42] During these "false alarms," you won't have access to your best thinking because your brain is focused on the danger.

The good news is there are things you can say and do to get your thinking brain back. We'll learn those soon, but first let's better understand what fight, flight, or freeze looks like.

[Share the information and visuals that follow below.]

Fight, Flight, or Freeze in "Real Time"

When students show the following behaviors, it is a sign they are in the throes of the stress response. They might be prone to one mode more than the other (I'm prone to freeze), or show a combination of the following:

Fight, Flight, Freeze

Fight: Act Out—argue, yell, say something nasty, hit, bite, throw, or break something

Flight: Escape—leave the room unannounced, wander, hide, or avoid people or situations such as school, a test, or performance

Freeze: Stuck—deer in the headlights, daydream, refuse to answer, play dead

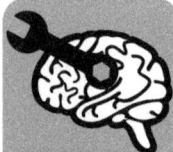

PRO TIP

"Thinking Brain" Hijack

When your students' stress response is activated, it impedes their ability to set goals, organize, plan, focus, get started, stick with a task, manage emotions, and reflect on how things are going. Their behavior, social interactions, motivation, mindset, effort, and confidence also suffer. In these moments, it's not the time to teach a lesson or coping strategy or ask kids to use their words," as the brain will have difficulty taking in, processing or retrieving old information or thinking critically.

Trauma and Adverse Childhood Experiences (ACEs)

Chronic stress, trauma, or Adverse Childhood Experiences (ACEs) impairs the healthy development of a child's EF. Drs. Vincent Felitti and Robert Anda led the ACE Study, asking more than 17,000 adults if they experienced any of the following between birth and their eighteenth birthday:[43]

- Physical, emotional, or sexual abuse
- Physical or emotional neglect
- Witness domestic violence
- Know an incarcerated relative
- Live with caregiver with untreated mental illness
- Live with caregiver with substance abuse
- Live through parents' divorce

Adults received a point toward their ACE score for each stressor they experienced; the higher the score, the greater the risk of health, social, and emotional challenges.

The following visual highlights the effects of trauma on health and well-being:

Adverse Childhood Experiences

Traumatic events that can have negative, lasting effects on health and wellbeing

Abuse
- Emotional abuse
- Physical abuse
- Sexual abuse

Neglect
- Emotional neglect
- Physical neglect

Household Challenges
- Domestic violence
- Substance abuse
- Mental illness
- Parental separation / divorce
- Incarcerated parent

People with 6+ ACEs can die

20 yrs

earlier than those who have none

1/8 of the population have more than 4 ACEs

www.70-30.org.uk
@7030Campaign

4 or more ACEs

3x the levels of lung disease and adult smoking

11x the level of intravenous drug abuse

14x the number of suicide attempts

4x as likely to have begun intercourse by age 15

4.5x more likely to develop depression

2x the level of liver disease

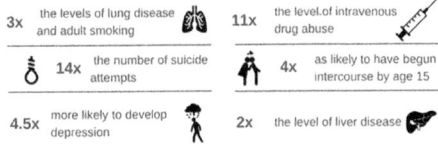

" Adverse childhood experiences are the single greatest unaddressed public health threat facing our nation today "

Dr. Robert Block, the former President of the American Academy of Pediatrics

67%
of the population have at least 1 ACE

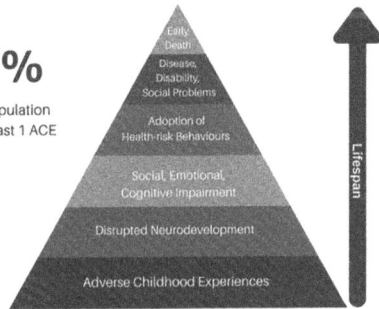

Pyramid (bottom to top):
- Adverse Childhood Experiences
- Disrupted Neurodevelopment
- Social, Emotional, Cognitive Impairment
- Adoption of Health-risk Behaviours
- Disease, Disability, Social Problems
- Early Death

Lifespan

Source: SFCCC.org

Kids experiencing ACEs are at higher risk for EF impairment during critical years of brain development when many executive skills are "coming online." These kids may have more EF gaps, resulting in challenges with academics, decision making, forethought, and hindsight; they can also exhibit behavior and disciplinary issues. You might know some kids who arrive at school on "high alert" even before learning has started. They may be worried about a family member's welfare, the safety of their neighborhood, or an uncertain situation at home. Other stressors such as immigration, racial violence, and inequity issues may also undermine attention, focus, and emotional regulation. Kids arriving at school in tears or acting guarded or withdrawn will be at higher risk for learning, emotional, and behavioral issues.

Not All Stress is Bad

With all that we've discussed about stress, you may think it has no redeeming qualities. Not true! A "little" stress can increase focus, alertness, and performance. It can motivate students to start their work, study for a test, or meet a deadline. Kids need to know it's okay to feel a bit nervous and still take the next step. However, there's a "sweet spot" when it comes to stress. A little can get students going on a task but too much can lead them to feel out of control or overwhelmed, which can activate the stress response.

What to Say to Lower Stress: Quick Language Scaffolds

Knowing the contagious effect of stress, the type of language and tone you use to talk about it can increase or decrease stress. Ask yourself, "Am I helping to lower or elevate the stress level?"

Kids need to know it's normal to feel anxious, frustrated, angry, bored, or confused from time to time. They also need to know how to label these feelings and take actions to feel better. As psychiatrist Dan Siegel says, "Name it to tame it."[44]

The following language scaffolds are designed to help kids (and adults):

- identify and express emotions in productive ways
- boost self-awareness, communication, and emotional development
- de-escalate stress, decrease behavior issues, and keep EF online

"Of Course… And…"

When kids or adults feel stressed, you may hear words that add drama and emotion to a situation. This can escalate stress, especially when the language supports avoidance, worst case outcomes, inflexibility, all-or-none thinking, or belief that things can't change. Here are some examples:

- "This is going to be a **disaster**! I'm going to look like a **loser**." (catastrophic)
- "**Everyone** but me knows how to do this. I'll **never** get it." (all/none, permanence)
- "I'm the **worst. I always** mess up!" (catastrophic, all/none)

When kids say the aforementioned comments (or something similar), it can hijack their "thinking brain," and we know what happens then!

To reduce stress levels, try responding with the words "of course…and…" Psychotherapist, anxiety specialist, and author Lynn Lyons introduced me to this simple and effective language tweak. "**Of course…**" sends a message of validation and empathy; "**and…**" sends a message of forward movement or next steps.

- When kids say, "I'll never get this." You can say, "**Of course,** something new can be hard, **and** you can do hard things."
- When kids say, "I'm afraid to try something new." You can say, "**Of course,** change can feel uncomfortable, **and** you can feel nervous and move forward at the same time."

Your Turn!

Reframe the following student comment with the "**Of course... and...**" technique:

When kids say, "I always mess up!" you can say, Of course_____, and _____.

Language About Failure

Many kids are afraid to raise their hands in class for fear of looking inept or unprepared. Others are stuck in perfectionism and think mistakes are signs they don't measure up. You can help kids lower their "mistake fear" and view failure in more productive ways by cultivating environments where mistakes are viewed as opportunities instead of obstacles.

How?

Begin by looking at *how you talk* about learning and failure. Kids need to know real learning takes time and effort. Mistakes *will* be part of the learning process, and the following acronym supports this kind of thinking.[45] I recommend posting and referencing it, especially when kids are learning something new.

FAIL:

F-first   **A**-attempts   **I**-in   **L**-learning

When providing feedback about your students' work, be mindful of the type of praise you use. For example:

- Instead of saying, "That's perfect!" ask, "How did you do that?" (Focus on process, not outcome.)

- Instead of saying, "You did that so fast!" say, "I'd like to give you something that actually challenges you." (We don't learn as much when we stick with something easy.)

Building Better Communication and Mindsets

Ineffective vs. Effective Communication

Wouldn't it be great if saying, "Don't worry about it," "Calm down," or "You're fine" actually helped? How have these worked for you in the past? Probably not so great. Here's why.

When we use language like the samples on the left side of the following chart, we send messages of dismissal, judgment, and shame. These ineffective (yet frequently used) comments don't typically lower stress or build skills. Often, they do the opposite!

The comments on the right side of the chart focus on validation, empathy, and problem-solving, which can decrease stress. When you validate how someone feels, it doesn't necessarily mean you agree; it just means you've listened, and this can put kids in a better mindset to try a strategy or new approach. [46]

INEFFECTIVE *Instead of saying…*	EFFECTIVE *Try saying…*
"Calm down," or "Don't worry."	"That sounds hard. I'm glad you're sharing."
"What do *you* have to worry about?" or "You're worried about *that*?"	"It sounds like part of you doesn't feel comfortable with…"
"Get over it!" or "You're fine."	"I can see you're trying to figure this out…need any help?"

What also helps:

Brief, objective, non-emotional language such as:

- "Hmmmm…"
- "I've noticed…"
- "Tell me more."

What doesn't help:

- Nagging
- Lectures
- Labeling
- Statements like: "You don't get it!", "You're not listening!", "If you only applied yourself!"
- Penalizing students for lacking skills

Growth Mindset

Carol Dweck's groundbreaking book *Mindset: The New Psychology of Success*, has direct applications for educators, counselors, coaches, and parents. Dweck's research supports the belief that a **growth mindset** can be developed with practice, effort, and training. Setbacks or challenges are opportunities for growth that build resilience and confidence. On the flip side, a **fixed mindset** is the belief that talents, intelligence, and personality are carved in stone. Hard work, practice, or feedback aren't highly valued.[47]

Mindset work pairs well with the aforementioned ways of reframing language as well as earlier discussions about neuroplasticity, change, practice, and failure. Here are some mindset activities to try with a partner or group:

LOOKS LIKE	SOUNDS LIKE	FEELS LIKE
• Think of people (real or fictional) who devote great effort to their work, embrace challenges, and are committed to improvement. • Read stories and watch videos, interviews, or movies about innovators, artists, writers, athletes, actors, etc. who dealt with failure and overcame setbacks. • Discuss, write, draw, or make a video about these people.	• Provide examples of the differences between a fixed and growth mindset. Ask kids which ones "sound like them." • Encourage kids to notice when their fixed mindset voice surfaces and teach how to reframe these thoughts to a growth mindset. • Practice growth mindset ways of talking, using language such as: effort, resilience, change, metacognition, plan, feedback, growth, hard work, etc.	• Describe something you did this week that was hard. What did you do that helped? • If you made a mistake or something didn't go well, did you take responsibility or blame others? Explain. • Think of people who challenge(d) the myth of the "natural" student or athlete. What helped them succeed? Think of "natural" athletes or students who didn't succeed as expected. What inhibited their success?[48]

Kids have a choice in how they view challenges, setbacks, and feedback. As shown in the chart that follows, the language used to talk about obstacles and mistakes sounds very different. If interpreted in a fixed mindset, kids may think they lack talent or ability. If viewed from a growth mindset, they may increase their effort and adjust their approach. A growth mindset helps kids persevere when they are disheartened about a grade, roadblock, or mistake. As international educational consultant and author Kathleen Kryza says, "Mindsets + Skill Sets = Results!"[49]

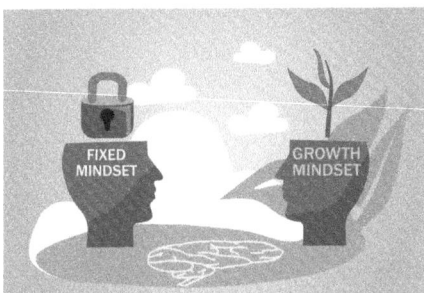

| FIXED MINDSET | GROWTH MINDSET |
Instead of saying…	*Try saying…*
"I'm afraid to try something new/hard."	"My brain gets stronger when I challenge it."
"If I don't get it right away, I'll quit."	"Learning takes time, effort, and patience."
"I can't make mistakes."	"I'll know how to do this better next time."
"Uggghh! I can't do this!"	"This is hard, and I'll improve with practice."
"It bothers me how my friend is so good at _____."	"Hmmm…maybe I can learn from my friend's approach."

Post visuals of growth mindset language, practice the mantras out loud (which may feel weird at first), and explore your mindset about yourself and student(s). Do you see yourself and kids as works in progress? What are some ways you'd like to grow in your profession or parenting? Growth mindset isn't about perfection—it's about being open to improvement. Kids know when we "walk the walk."

What to Do to Decrease Stress: Quick Resets

There may be times in which you are working with stressed colleagues, kids, or parents and find yourself feeling overwhelmed or anxious. Research indicates that educator wellness correlates to fewer behavior issues and better school climates, job satisfaction, and academic outcomes.[50] So much starts with you.

The following reset tools can be used with kids and adults to combat stress and trauma collaboratively:

Slow, Deep Breathing

- You and your students always have slow, deep breathing at your disposal to regulate the nervous system. You can pair 4/6 breathing (mentioned earlier in the chapter) with some of your favorite breathing practices.

- Dr. Chris Willard, a clinical psychologist specializing in mindfulness and coauthor of *Alphabreaths: The ABCs of Mindful Breathing*, encourages kids to make up their own breathing practice and teach it to a friend or class. With kids doing "more of the thinking," they're more likely to use these techniques independently in real time to help themselves or a friend.

Movement

One way to expel excess energy or distract someone from their worries is to engage in movement. Consider these options:

A Mindful Walk

Focus on each sense for about a minute: How many things can you see? Hear? Feel? Smell? Taste?

Wall Pushups

- Face wall, arms-length away
- Place hands on wall, shoulder-width apart
- Bend elbows and lean into wall
- Hold position for one second
- Slowly push back until arms are straight, then repeat

Chair Yoga Poses

Sit tall, breathe slow (Mountain Pose).	Reach arms overhead, crisscross forearms (Eagle Arms).	Arch back, then round back (Cat-Cow).	Stand near chair, lift one foot (Tree Pose with support).

Stress Spots

When kids experience stress in their bodies, it can be loud and messy! The mind and body work in sync, and when the mind is full of worried, frustrated, or angry thoughts, we might feel tightness, tingling, stomachaches, headaches, sweaty palms, a fast heartbeat, or even diarrhea.

To help kids notice their body's warning signs, you can use the **Stress Spots Worksheet**. Ask them to imagine the image on the paper as their body and to make a dot wherever they feel stress. Next, use the prompts to help kids identify physiological sensations and action steps to reduce the body's stress.

Counting Colors

Try this mindful practice to promote visual awareness and quiet the mind:

1. Look around the room and see if you can silently find five things that are blue. (Take about 15 seconds.)

2. Continue in the same manner. Find four things that are red, three things that are yellow, two things that are green, and one thing that is purple, taking 15 seconds for each. (Choose colors of your choice).

3. Let's take a deep, slow breath. Now, bring your focus back to me (or your work). [51]

Mindful Snack/Drink

When students dial into their senses, it can distract them from their worries. Snack time is an opportunity to ask kids to focus on sensory sensations such as:

- flavors (Is it tart, spicy, or sweet?)
- temperature (Is it warm or cold?)
- texture (Is it crunchy or smooth?)

The ABC Strategy

The three-step approach from *ABC Worry Free* validates students' worries, cues their nervous system to "pump the brakes," and reframes how they think about their worry. This strategy is an effort to interrupt the stress response and send the message, "You're okay and can handle the situation, despite feeling uncertain or uncomfortable."

You can apply the strategy to any distressing thought such as:

Math Example

- **A=Accept** (Math is hard for me.)
- **B=Breathe** (Do 4/6 breathing to calm myself.)
- **C=Change my thinking** (Turn a threat into opportunity or new way of thinking: "Real learning isn't quick or easy. I'll highlight keywords, take it step by step, and remind myself that I can do hard things!")

Post a variety of samples of the ABC Strategy so that kids see they're not alone in their worries or frustrations, and they can do something productive to manage them.

Here's a sample lesson using the book, snow globe, and **Stress Spots Worksheet** activities:

ABC Worry Free: Sample Lesson

- Warm Up: Snow Globe activity
- Quick Write or Draw: What worries you?
- Stress Spots: Where you feel worry
- Read story
- Discuss the story
- Exit Card: How can you use Max's "trick" for something that worries you?

Source: Noel Foy, Neuro Noel Consulting © 2024

Common Behaviors: What Are They Telling Us?

When your students are dealing with high stress, experiencing cognitive overload, or lacking the proficiency needed to complete a task (or all these), you may notice the following behaviors, which can communicate you are "losing" your students (or are about to):

- Heads on desk
- Eyes glazed over
- Irritated/restless/antsy/withdrawn
- Slouching in chairs
- Staring out the window
- On their phone (texting, scrolling)
- Talking to others while you're talking
- Acting like a class clown

Instead of labeling these students as underperformers or "bad" kids, ask what these behaviors tell us about student(s)' stress levels, skill gaps, and what's being done to support them. When you notice these signs, pause, notice the language you're using, and do a quick reset. This might feel counter-intuitive, given all the work that might need completing. Yet, here's the reality: if your students aren't taking in the information, they won't have it at their disposal for later access. It's more productive to reset and get their "thinking brain" in charge.

Student Story

John, a high school junior with performance anxiety related to test taking and sports, was at his wit's end. He was often told how smart and talented he was, but he didn't feel that way. He studied for tests and trained for baseball, but he'd blank out on exams and freeze when it was his turn at bat, despite being one of the best athletes on the team.

As the school year and baseball season progressed, John became more hopeless and reactive. His confidence was waning, his focus in class was inconsistent, and he didn't believe there was much he could do to turn things around academically and athletically. Playoffs and PSAT's were looming, and John was stressing about disappointing his parents and team.

One of the first things I noticed was John's mindset and use of language that reinforced catastrophic, permanent, and all-or-none thinking. If he didn't turn things around, he believed no college would accept him. If he performed well in school or sports, he considered himself "the man." If not, he was a "loser."

Given what we've discussed, what might support John?

We worked on the difference between a growth and fixed mindset. He learned how to reframe his stressors with the ABC Strategy and "Of course…and…" frames, which helped him better manage adversity. He was able to replace his catastrophic thinking with growth mindset thoughts and not allow his worries to "freak him out."

I also taught John about neuroplasticity, his brain, the stress response, how his EF gets hijacked, and how to reset. He found the mind/body check, 4/6 breathing, quick resets, and language about failure helpful, and he applied them during classes, homework, tests, and baseball. He now noticed his warning signs and took steps to "slow the game down." Additionally, I coached his parents about the aforementioned concepts as well as how to respond to him.

When John took the PSAT's, he used his strategies in real time to manage his anxiety, and he produced favorable results. He was better able to concentrate in class, complete homework efficiently, plan out long-term assignments, start them earlier, and ask clarifying questions. John was pleased with his progress and ability to produce in performance-related situations.

QUESTIONS to CONSIDER

1. Describe a time when anger, anxiety, frustration, boredom, or lack or relevance interfered with your learning or performance.

2. What real or perceived threats activate your students' stress responses? What do their behaviors look like, and how do they "reset" themselves?

3. What do you teach your students about the impact of stress on learning? How do you foresee using the language scaffolds and quick resets in this chapter to your advantage?

4. Does every student you work with feel you believe in them? If not, what might help?

KEY POINTS

- The brain doesn't discern between real or perceived threats and may experience stress as anxiety, frustration, anger, boredom, and lack of relevance.

- High stress can activate the stress response and hijack EF, resulting in kids who might act out, zone out, or feel stuck.

- Chronic stress, trauma, or ACEs can impair healthy development of EF and put kids at high risk for learning, emotional, and behavioral issues.

- The language frames and reset responses in this chapter are designed to prevent the emotional brain from hijacking the "thinking brain."

4 More of Them, Less of You

The brain that does the work does the learning.

Dr. Mel Riddle

Resist the Urge to Be Kids' Pre-Frontal Cortex

I'm so fond of Riddle's quote I often ask my students and workshop participants to repeat it out loud. It reminds kids to own their part in the learning process and reminds educators and parents to refrain from doing too much of the "thinking, talking, or doing" for students.

When kids struggle with EF, your instinct might be to step in and help. However, stepping in too soon or often can promote learned helplessness and accustom kids to habits in which they don't do much thinking or self-advocating. Instead, focus on skill-building and incrementally releasing more responsibility to students. It's easy to *unintentionally* fall into the trap of doing too much of the thinking and problem-solving. Resist being their pre-frontal cortex!

Kids need environments that normalize and value challenges, so they can flex their "productive struggle" muscles and "get comfortable with some discomfort," especially when they make mistakes or face uncertainty or adversity. I remember my anxiety showing up when my sons and students struggled. Yet, *allowing* them to make mistakes and do more of the thinking and processing decreased their sense of helplessness and increased their confidence and autonomy.

Getting students to take ownership of their learning can be challenging. You might be tempted to do their work (i.e., finish a paragraph, pack up backpacks, wake up teenagers), thinking it's a quicker solution. In the short term, you might be right. However, this can inadvertently deny students of much needed skill-building practice. In the long term, removing any discomfort or struggle doesn't increase stamina or resilience. Instead, it delays growth and EF skill development, adding more work to your plate and keeping you in an incessant (and often stressful) loop.

When your kids are learning skills or completing tasks, ask yourself,

"Who's doing most of the thinking, processing, and talking?"

If it's you, *you* are doing the learning instead of the kids.

When you ask students to complete a task or assignment, you likely envision the "finished product," but kids with executive dysfunction typically don't. Whether writing an essay, tidying up their desk, or transitioning to the next activity, they might lack a clear picture in their mind of the expectations and steps. If they do, *it's usually not the same vision as yours, and they may have another way of "getting there."* When students have difficulty visualizing themselves doing a task, it can lead to procrastination or behavior issues. It's hard for kids to know what they're working toward if they don't know where they're going.

Ways to Boost Metacognition

Be Intentional and Transparent

If you were to ask your students why they use a certain graphic organizer, template, or strategy, what would they say?

During my classroom observations, I ask students that question. If they say, "Because my teacher likes it," their response lacks metacognition, and I doubt they'll use the strategy independently. On the other hand, if students say, "This graphic organizer helps me brainstorm and sequence my thoughts," I know they understand its purpose and may use it again.

If your students can't tell you why they're using something, they're probably not experiencing much benefit or transfer value. To combat this, Kathleen Kyrza recommends the following:

- **Be Intentional:** *you know why* you're using a particular strategy or template.
- **Be Transparent:** *the kids know and can express why* they're using it.[52]

Your Turn!

Ask your students to explain the "why" behind a template, graphic organizer, or strategy you use with them. If their responses don't reflect that they understand its purpose, how can you be more intentional and transparent?

Build a Mental Blueprint with Future Glasses

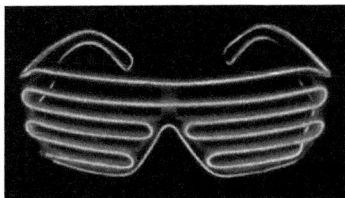

Developed by Sarah Ward and Kristen Jacobsen, this metacognitive strategy works well for tasks or processes (i.e., transitions, homework routines, classroom norms, assignments, labs). When you ask students to wear their "future glasses," they begin to visualize the future and develop a mental schema of the finished product, planning, and necessary steps.

To boost students' working memory and help them build a mental blueprint, ask:

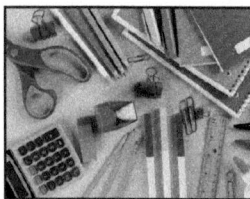

"When you picture yourself doing (or getting ready for _____, what do you see?" [53]

(i.e., a task or process)

If students say, "I don't know what to do or I don't picture much," that's okay. Their responses reveal where they are in their thinking and skill development. To help them better "see" each step, provide visual cues with the following questions:

Build A Mental Blueprint

What do I need?

Where am I going to work?

When will I start? How long will I be there?

Who can I ask for help?

When teaching about future glasses, you can don an actual pair of sunglasses or just imagine doing so. I typically wear a wacky pair of sunglasses to ramp up the fun meter and gets kids' attention, which may seem like something suited for younger kids, but older students enjoy the novelty, too. Besides, why should the younger kids have all the fun?

Meta Talk at Each Stage of Learning

Meta Talk pairs well with Future Glasses and involves asking questions before, during, and after a task, activity, or process. Hearing and saying these mind rehearsal questions aid working memory and help "flex the muscles" that support learning, planning, organizing, prioritizing, predicting, time management, self-monitoring, self-regulation, and growth mindset.

Questions can be answered individually or with a partner via Think-Pair-Shares, Write-Pair-Shares, Draw-Pair-Shares, Do Now's or Exit Tickets, typically taking 3 minutes or less.

Here's what Meta Talk looks and sounds like:

Meta Talk at Each Stage of Learning

Before: Make a Plan	During: Self-Monitor	After: Evaluate
• What am I doing or learning? • What is my goal?	• How is the process going? • Do I need to make some adjustments?	• Did I submit my work? • Did I reach my goal? Why/why not?
• What have I done before like this? • Who will I work with or ask for help?	• How does this feel? • If I'm stuck, what can I say or do to help?	• Next time I will_____. • I realize I do better when I _____.
• What is my plan (steps, materials, where I'll work, when I'll start, etc.)?	• I get/did _____, but need to work more on_____.	• I did it! I didn't know _____ before, but now I can_____.

Meta Talk helps kids better understand how they learn, boosting their self-awareness and ownership. They begin to realize one's approach and planning matter. For example, students might recognize they remember more of what they read when they use reading strategies, experience more success with writing when they apply a writing process, or are more productive when they do homework in a quiet room instead of in front of the television.

As students incrementally do more of the thinking and processing, you'll notice them shift from feeling helpless to empowered, which means less work for you! Encourage students to apply their newfound metacognitive thinking to experiences beyond academics, although skill transfer to new situations doesn't typically happen automatically for kids with EF issues. They will likely need support brainstorming and discussing other scenarios in which Meta Talk can help (i.e., social situations, extracurriculars, personal development).

Your Turn!
How do you foresee using the Meta Talk questions/prompts? Are there any others you'd add?

Tell vs. Ask

When you tell students what to do, you're doing the thinking. Asking them questions requires more brain power on their part and provides practice with problem solving and taking action. This increases confidence, responsibility, and independence. Notice the difference in these examples:[54]

TELL	ASK
• Get going on your work.	• What is your plan to get started?
• Go chill out.	• What can you do to get unstuck?
• Here's your grade.	• What worked well? What would you change next time?
• Get your backpack.	• What strategy might help you remember your school gear?

Title Talk

This simple trick helps kids take ownership of tasks. Here's how it works: take a task and turn it into a job title. For example, instead of saying, "Start your homework," say, "You're a homework starter!" This shift helps kids tap their thinking skills about the task's requirements versus making excuses to avoid it, while increasing motivation, confidence, and a positive sense of self.[55] Give it a go and see what happens!

Telling Approach	Job Title Approach
• Clean your room.	• You're a room organizer!
• Pay attention.	• Time to be a listener!
• Organize your backpack.	• You're a backpack organizer!
• You need to begin.	• Time to be a task initiator!

Make Learning Environments "No PEE Zones"

Forgive my use of potty talk. I can hear you chuckling, "What the heck is a PEE zone?" It's the antithesis of a brain-appealing learning environment!

I was introduced to the PEE model from my colleague Becky who learned it from her mentor Erlene Minton. In a PEE zone, instructors:

- **<u>P</u>RESENT** subject matter
- **<u>E</u>XPLAIN** it
- **<u>E</u>XPECT** students to understand and know how to use the information

To better picture a PEE zone, visualize the epic scene from *Ferris Bueller's Day Off* in which the monotone teacher delivers a painfully boring history lesson but doesn't make adjustments, despite clearly "losing" his students. "Anyone? Anyone?" Yep, a bona fide PEE Zone, one that's still widely used today. Heavy on *you*, light on *them.*

Students in PEE zones are often asked, "Everyone understand?" despite the clues and cues that several students didn't understand what was being taught. Students often nod in glum agreement, teachers move on, and comprehension gaps increase. Little time (if any) is given to paired or group interactions to practice the subject matter, make meaningful connections, think critically, learn from mistakes, or implement feedback. These are essential components to developing competence, confidence, and independence.

I'm not confident the PEE model will sufficiently develop EF in kids and prepare them for the top skills needed for college, career, and life readiness. Are you?

Reduce Teacher Talk, Increase Student Learning

If I asked you to estimate the percentage of time you talk vs. your students during a lesson or meeting, what would that ratio be?

John Hattie, author of *Visible Learning for Teachers,* found that teachers talk 70-80% of class time, reaching 89% in some classrooms. He concludes, "...teachers should talk less and think more carefully about when they're talking and the kinds of questions they're asking." Hattie challenges us to ask, "How can we assess and hear the impact of our teaching if we're doing most of the talking?"[56]

In that vein, habitually ask yourself, "To what extent are the kids doing the thinking and talking? What skills are they practicing?" Teacher-directed lessons, especially if boring, will be harder for kids with EF challenges and

ADHD to stay attentive, focused, and engaged. Kids with ADHD are paying attention but *often not to what we want them to*!

To increase focus, engagement, and academic risk-taking for *all* students instead of only the "smart kids," the following cooperative learning strategies can help kids process and talk about information with a partner or group (I also find they boost comprehension and test scores). Asking a combination of low and high-level questions, I aim for a mix of these "moves" throughout a lesson (about one for every 10 minute "chunk" of instruction):

Think-Pair-Share

- **THINK:** Ask students a question about a text, concept, skill, etc. Provide 15-30 seconds of "think time."
- **PAIR:** Pair students with a partner.
- **SHARE:** Students share their thoughts with a partner.

Write-Pair-Share or Draw-Pair-Share

Follow the same steps for a Think-Pair-Share, expect after giving students "think time," ask them to do a Quick Write or Quick Draw in response to the question you pose (about 2 minutes).

> **Your Turn!**
> Do you notice any PEE-ing in your instruction? How might you incorporate Think-Pair-Shares (or Write or Draw-Pair-Shares) to promote "less of you, more of them?"

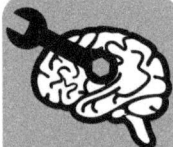

Engagement Boosters

- Your neurodivergent learners may need extra "think time" or "wait time" to answer questions you pose.
- To avoid one student from dominating a conversation, give each student about 30 seconds to talk. Say, "Talk to the person on the left. Go!" Set a timer for 30 seconds and sound a chime after time's up. Continue the same step for the person on the right. Then, ask students to share what they discussed with the class.
- Instead of agreeing or telling students they did a good job, ask questions like: "Can you build on that comment?", "What evidence supports it?", or "Do you agree or disagree? Why?"

Retrieval Strategies: How To Be a "Golden" Retriever

We've addressed strategies that enhance the first two stages of learning:

- getting the information into your students' brains (encoding)
- helping it stick (storage).

Now, we're ready for the third stage: getting it out (retrieval).[57]

To get information from working memory to long term storage, we must do something with it, and what better way to retrieve information than with retrieval strategies! I'm such a fan because they're quick, don't need grading, and can be easily integrated into various settings. Moreover, they're low on stress but high on learning. Instead of reminding kids what to remember, students recall what they've learned, providing "real time" formative assessments of what's sticking, missing, or confusing. (Yep, more of them, less of you!)

Retrieval practices also facilitate the development of executive function by reinforcing:

- metacognition and awareness of how to learn
- engagement and attention
- mental organization of knowledge
- retention of information over the long term
- higher order thinking and transfer of knowledge
- preparation for class and exams

Pooja K. Agarwal and Patrice M. Bain discuss various retrieval practices and how to use them in their book *Powerful Teaching*.[58] Here are three of my favorites, which I have modified slightly:

Brain Dump

1. Pause a lesson, lecture, or activity at mid-point or after teaching a concept or introducing new information.
2. Ask students to write down in a notebook (to be used regularly) what they remember (60-90 seconds). You want kids to save their lists. (You'll soon see why.)
3. Ask students to share with a partner (about 30 seconds each).

Bam! You now have a quick gauge of what students recalled. With that instant feedback, you can clear up any misinformation or confusion.

You can take a Brain Dump a few steps further. After students finish their list, ask them to check their notes for anything important they missed (about 1-2 minutes). If in a group setting, students can Pair Share and add something new to their Brain Dump from their partner's list. You can then ask, "What's something both of you wrote?"

Your Turn!
Do a one-minute Brain Dump on anything you've learned in this book. Go!

Three Things and a Question

1. At the end of a class or session, ask students to write down three key things they learned, along with one question regarding something they're wondering about or need to clarify. Have kids save their responses in a notebook they'll use again.

2. You can move on from here or follow step 3 from the Brain Dump.

Your Turn!
What are three important points in this book?
What is a question you might have?

Learning Quiz

I was that kid who dreaded pop quizzes. I realize now I would have benefited from taking them regularly instead of sporadically. What I remember most was an air of judgment and high stakes—the focus was on the grade, not the learning.

With a Learning Quiz, the focus is on...dah, the learning! Kids do the thinking and use information from their earlier Brain Dumps and Three Things and a Question to generate their quizzes (or their own study guides). When kids realize they will revisit and repurpose their previous notes, they will value them more.

I'm not wild about teacher-made review sheets, because who's doing the thinking about what's important? Yep, you. While retrieval practices are not summative assessments, they are effective learning tools to get kids doing more, so you can do less!

Here's how your students can make a Learning Quiz:

1. Refer to previous Brain Dumps and/or Three Things and a Question from a section.

2. Make up 3-5 questions (i.e., fill in the blank, T/F, multiple choice, short answer) on key terms, vocabulary, and concepts.

3. Have students take their own or a partner's quiz (could be done as a warm-up or exit ticket).

> **Your Turn!**
> Using your previous Brain Dump and Three Things and a Question, make a Learning Quiz for yourself (or someone else who read this book).

Reflection

From my experience using these and previously-mentioned strategies, I get more out of my students and see a boost in participation, engagement, metacognition, retention, motivation, EF, and SEL with less stress and behavior issues. Along with teachers I work with, I notice up to a 20% increase on academic assessments, particularly for the strugglers. I also see improvement with positive self-talk, collaboration, overcoming obstacles, and being receptive to feedback.

Self-Monitoring

When kids take a step back, observe how something is going, and reflect on how it ended, they learn to evaluate their behavior, skills, and performance. By thinking about their goals, approaches, or what they need to do differently next time, kids boost their ownership and metacognition. They also begin to notice the connection of effort to progress. Many kids are weak in these areas, and without self-assessment, they'll likely repeat the same mistakes again and miss valuable practice with foresight and hindsight.

When teaching kids to self-assess, be intentional and transparent! Using checklists or rubrics, kids can self- or peer-assess their use of Meta Talk, learning goals, and strategies.

Here are some self-assessments I use with students to help them "course correct" in real time:

Five Steps to Success

This tool gets kids thinking about their goals, plan for learning, and the behaviors they'll need to succeed. During classroom visits, I'll ask kids, "What are you learning?" I'm astounded at how often they respond, "I don't know." You can help kids self-monitor their learning right out of the gate by asking ALL students to say the learning objective(s) out loud (hopefully it's on the board) versus asking just one student to do so. If students don't know what they're learning, how can we expect them to monitor their progress?

Top Three Hits

To help kids avoid making repeated errors on homework, writing tasks, and tests, you can utilize the strategy from SMARTS' Executive Function Curriculum. It is designed to teach students how to prioritize and self-check their work by having them identify and correct their most common mistakes ("Top 3 Hits"). [59]

How Am I Doing?

Teaching students to objectively review their approach to work is a valuable skill they can use throughout their school journey and chosen career paths. Doing so gives them a sense of "where they are" in their skill-building process and reinforces the power of practice.

Using the **How Am I Doing? Checklist**, ask students to rate their proficiency and use of strategies.

The following example applies to a writing task:

Student Story

When Maeve's mom asked me to work with her daughter, I could hear the panic in her voice. Maeve had just finished her freshman year of college, and it hadn't gone well. She was on academic probation, prompting her parents to have Maeve tested. She was diagnosed with ADHD, inattentive type, which helped explain why Maeve had trouble with organization, focus, task initiation, and deadlines. She had no system for notetaking or time management, which led her to feel overwhelmed, get behind, and eventually give up.

Maeve was feeling down on herself for her lack of autonomy, systems, and strategies. However, she wanted to stress less, develop new habits, and learn about EF and how it interfered with her success academically and socially. Maeve was especially motivated, as she planned to apply to a master's program. I began by helping her and her parents understand the testing results and asked each to consider their responsibilities in this process.

Given what we've discussed, what might support Maeve?

A top priority was finding a quiet place for Maeve to study. In the past, she'd get distracted, socialize, and lose track of time. Future Glasses and Meta Talk were game changers—she now pictured and planned where, when, and how she'd approach studying. She noticed several Time Thieves getting in the way of her efficiency and devised a remedy for each. She did movement breaks when antsy or tired and put her phone in her bag if it distracted her. If she felt anxious, she'd do 4/6 breathing. If she didn't know how to start something, she'd ask a friend or teacher for help.

Maeve responded well to the Mind-Body Check, breathing practices, and discussions about neuroplasticity. She began to believe in the possibility of change and became better at managing stress. Maeve found "Of Course… and… ", the ABC Strategy, and Growth Mindset reframes helpful for managing anxiety and non-productive thoughts or perspectives. We started our sessions with a retrieval strategy, which helped Maeve review concepts, see what was sticking, and identify what needed more work. She also applied retrieval strategies in her classes and followed a notetaking system and writing process. Maeve now used a calendar to record deadlines and a daily planner for appointments, meetings, and daily tasks.

Through coaching Maeve's parents, they realized their well-intended efforts had inadvertently developed into habits of doing too much of the "thinking, talking, and doing" for their daughter. By gaining a deeper understanding of EF and their role in the process, they better communicated with Maeve (using language scaffolds, Tell vs. Ask, Meta Talk, etc.). These language shifts were hard at first, but they kept working at it in hopes that Maeve would take more ownership of her life.

Maeve also needed support applying these strategies outside of school (i.e., driving, nights out with friends, and transitioning from college to home without falling into old patterns). With regular self-monitoring and weekly meetings throughout the semester, Maeve stayed on top of her work, effectively managed stress, and achieved success in her classes.

1. If you notice yourself doing too much of the "thinking, talking, and doing," what strategies from this chapter might help?

2. How do your expectations of a "finished product" match with your students' expectations? Which of the metacognitive strategies and language can you see yourself using?

3. How might you incorporate retrieval or self-monitoring practices with your students?

KEY POINTS

- Doing too much of the thinking and problem-solving for kids can lead to learned helplessness, which delays growth and deprives them of skill-building opportunities.

- Rather than tell students what to do, cue their brains on how to do something by using visuals, verbal cues, or problem-solving prompts that promote metacognition.

- When offering help to students, ask yourself, "Who's doing the thinking and processing? What type of skill-building is involved?"

- When students develop a better understanding of how they learn, it increases their self-awareness, metacognition, and ownership.

- Meta Talk allows students to "see" and "hear" the language of each step of learning and rehearse in their minds what they need to do before actually doing it.

- Retrieval practices provide formative assessments on what kids recall from the information they've learned.

Brain-Appealing, Dopamine-Friendly Environments

5

*If you're not modeling what you're teaching,
you're teaching something else.*

Martha Tate

Kids need to believe that what you are teaching is important and can add value to their lives. Your enthusiasm goes a long way in setting the tone, as does the right amount of structure, scaffolding, and engagement. When students are in what Judy Wills calls their "achievable challenge" range and believe they are competent to do what you have asked, their stress levels and behavior problems decrease while EF, critical thinking, engagement, and ownership increase.

Kids are naturally curious about the world around them, yet their curiosity and enthusiasm for learning often wanes in school. This bums me out, but I have hope for change. Exciting discoveries about learning and the brain have direct applications in and beyond the classroom, which you can use to your advantage to boost EF and inform lesson design and learning experiences. Here's how!

Be a Dopamine Conduit

You probably know your brain is a pleasure-seeking organ that releases dopamine when it does something pleasurable. Are you taking advantage of that knowledge? Ask yourself, "Do your students arrive at your class or meetings with a sense of curiosity? Or dread or indifference?" If the latter, try integrating more dopamine-filled approaches into the learning process, and watch what happens! When kids experience a dopamine boost from an enjoyable activity, it decreases stress and boosts academic success and EF, particularly regarding:

- Attention
- Focus
- Memory
- Motivation
- Persistence/Perseverance[60]

Wowza! Knowing the role of dopamine (just the *expectation* of a dopamine reward can be motivating), it behooves us to incorporate experiences that keep it flowing, especially given that students with ADHD may have lower levels of dopamine. In the majority of classrooms, less than half of the students are paying attention to the lesson.[61] When kids aren't paying attention, they're more likely to misbehave, and if kids are not focused on the lesson, how are they expected to remember and learn?

Seeing that the brain prioritizes dopamine-filled experiences, you have a better chance of getting kids' attention when you incorporate them. Once you have their attention, information begins its journey to the "thinking brain" before making its way past the amygdala, the brain's emotional center. If a learning experience seems threatening, information will divert from the thinking brain to activate the fight, flight, or freeze response. Willis explains, "When your child is stressed, the amygdala directs information to the *reactive* non-thinking brain. When your child is relaxed, comfortable and interested, the amygdala directs the information to the *reflective*, thinking brain."[62]

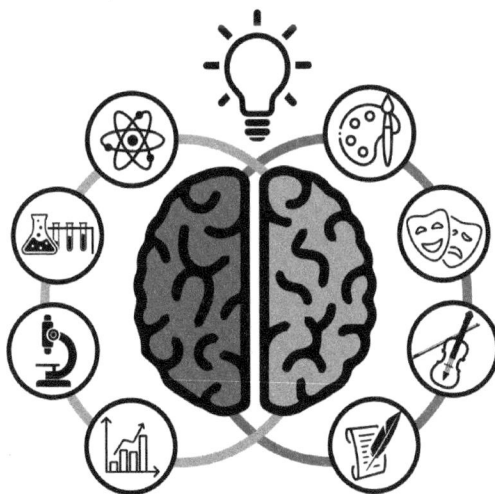

Target Different Modalities

Source: Edmunton Blog

Since we learn with our senses, students will select sensory information from their environment that gets their attention. Just as animals pay attention to sensory input and details in their environment to form memories and survive (Where are the dangerous or safe places to eat or rest?), so do your students.[63] If your students recall an experience from a class or situation that productively engaged their senses and interests, they'll likely come back for more. If it wasn't enjoyable or safe, they may avoid it, act out, or "play dead."

Knowing this, you might better appreciate why we spent Chapter 3 on the impact of stress and what you can do to lower it. When stress is high, dopamine drops, learning goes down, and information won't reach the thinking brain. A positive learning climate and prevention of stressors help information pass through the amygdala to the pre-frontal cortex, which leads to more smiles, joy, and ownership of learning. You'll hear kids say, "Can we do this again?"

Isn't that what we want?

To maximize the dopamine effect, incorporate more of what the brain likes into learning experiences:[64]

BRAIN BOOSTERS CHEAT SHEET

SAFE, LOW THREAT CULTURE	Cultivate a low threat/high learning culture where all students are respected and mistakes are valued (this boosts academic risk-taking and builds hard and soft skills needed in careers/life).
NOVELTY	Pique curiosity and attention with something unexpected (i.e., walk backwards to show negative numbers, play content-based games, tell a story, share an anecdote, show "cool" videos or objects connected to "the learning").
PERSONAL RELEVANCE	Reinforce the "why" to what's being taught or done, be "intentional" and "transparent," set goals that connect to kids' goals/interests and include real-world applications.

MULTI-SENSORY LEARNING	Engage the brain to actively process in varied ways with multiple senses (i.e., pictures, images, graphic organizers, color coding, experiential learning, journaling, writing, drawing, pair shares, movement, singing, video-making).
ACHIEVABLE CHALLENGE	Find the "sweet spot" for "productive struggle." Work that's too easy=boredom; too hard=frustration. Differentiate instruction and be mindful of cognitive overload.
PHYSICAL MOVEMENT	Take short movement breaks and pair movement to learning (i.e., math concepts, writing process, vocabulary, etc.).
CHOICE	Allow choice of topic and audience for writing tasks and how to communicate ideas (i.e., drawing, writing, video, etc).
PREDICTIONS	Bulletin boards previewing "coming attractions;" make and change predictions (intrinsic satisfaction builds with accurate predictions).
OPTIMISM	Reinforce Growth Mindset and character-building thoughts/self-talk.
MUSIC	Choose songs that suit your purpose or theme (i.e., fast beat to increase energy and slow beat to calm).
HUMOR	Incorporate riddles/jokes related to the learning.
PRODUCTIVE BODY LANGUAGE	Standing/sitting straight with shoulders back sends confident messages to brain vs. slouching/head down.
WELL-BEING	Show mindful and compassionate care for self and others.
INQUIRY AND DISCOVERY	Promote curiosity and critical thinking with Bloom's Taxonomy
PRODUCTIVE PEER INTERACTIONS	Do polls or creative Think-Write-Draw-Pair Shares to engage and check for understanding (i.e., students take a "Learning Walk" or write a headline, tweet, or poem about key takeaways). Partner work can boost focus and accountability, especially for ADHD/EF issues.

Here's another handy cheat sheet to reference when you're looking for ways to boost executive function, engagement, and autonomy in your students. Similar to the Brain Boosters Cheat Sheet, the Executive Function Cheat Sheet reinforces several concepts, strategies, and activities featured throughout this book but aligns them to specific skills. Both sheets are designed for use in home, school, private practice, clinical settings and beyond, or when completing the Brain-Boosting Learning Plan to follow.

EXECUTIVE FUNCTION CHEAT SHEET

GOAL SETTING	• Chapter 1: Getting to Know Me, Skill Building Plan • Chapter 2: Schedule, Calendar, Planner, Homework Log • Chapter 4: Meta Talk • Chapter 4: 5 Steps to Success
PLANNING/ PRIORITIZING	• Chapter 2: Schedule, Calendar, Planner, Homework Log, Make Planning Visible • Chapter 4: Future Glasses, Meta Talk • Chapter 5: Match the Picture, Get Ready/Do/Done, STOP
ORGANIZATION	• Chapter 2: Notetaking, Writing Process, Schedule, Calendar, Planner, Make Planning Visible • Chapter 4: Future Glasses, Meta Talk • Chapter 5: Match the Picture, Get Ready/Do/Done, STOP
TASK INITIATION	• Chapter 2: Pomodoro Technique, Analog Clock, Schedule, Calendar, Planner • Chapter 4: Future Glasses, Meta Talk, Tell vs. Ask, Title Talk • Chapter 5: Match the Picture, Get Ready/Do/Done, STOP
TIME MANAGEMENT	• Chapter 2: Time Thieves, Analog Clock, Pomodoro Technique, Schedule, Calendar, Planner, Make Planning Visible, Homework Log • Chapter 4: Meta Talk • Chapter 5: Get Ready/Do/Done, STOP

WORKING MEMORY	• Chapter 2: Text Features and Structures, Comprehension Monitoring • Chapter 4: Intentional and Transparent, Future Glasses, Meta Talk, Tell vs. Ask, Title Talk, Retrieval Strategies (Brain Dump, Three Things and a Question, Learning Quiz) • Chapter 5: Match the Picture, Get Ready/Do/Done, STOP
FOCUS	• Chapter 2: Text Features and Structures, Comprehension Monitoring, Writing Process, Pomodoro Technique, Notetaking, Schedule, Calendar, Planner, Homework Log • Chapter 3: Mind/Body Check, Quick Resets (Slow, Deep Breathing, Mindful Walk or Snack, Wall Pushups, Chair Yoga, Counting Colors) • Chapter 4: Meta Talk, Tell vs. Ask, Title Talk, Think-Draw-Write Pair Shares • Chapter 5: Match the Picture, Get Ready/Do/Done, STOP
EFFORT/MINDSET	• Chapter 1: Best and Worst Learning Experiences • Chapter 2: Homework Log • Chapter 3: Mind/Body Check, Quick Resets (Slow, Deep Breathing, Mindful Walk, Wall Pushups, Chair Yoga), Language Scaffolds (Feel and Deal, "Of Course" & "And," FAIL, Fixed vs. Growth Mindset), Think-Draw-Write Pair Shares, correct mistakes • Chapter 4: Intentional and Transparent, Meta Talk, 5 Steps to Success • Chapter 5: Match the Picture, Get Ready/Do/Done, STOP
COGNITIVE FLEXIBILITY	• Chapter 2: Schedule, Calendar, Planner, Make Planning Visible, Transition Cues, Bloom's Taxonomy • Chapter 4: Meta Talk, Tell vs. Ask, Title Talk, Think-Draw-Write-Pair Shares • Chapter 5: STOP
RESPONSE INHIBITION	• Chapter 3: Mind/Body Check with 4/6 Breathing, Language Scaffolds (Feel and Deal, "Of Course" & "And") Fixed vs. Growth Mindset, Quick Resets (Slow, Deep Breathing, Mindful Walk) • Chapter 4: Future Glasses, Meta Talk, Tell vs. Ask, Title Talk • Chapter 5: Match the Picture, STOP to "Read the Room"

SELF-REGULATION	• Chapter 3: Mind/Body Check, Clear/Cloudy Brain and the Stress Response, Language Scaffolds (i.e., Feel and Deal, "Of Course" & "And," FAIL, Fixed vs. Growth Mindset), Quick Resets (Slow, Deep Breathing, Mindful Walk or Snack, Wall Pushups, Chair Yoga, Counting Colors, Stress Spots, ABC Strategy)
	• Chapter 4: Future Glasses, Meta Talk, Title Talk, Tell vs. Ask
	• Chapter 5: Match the Picture, STOP
SELF-MONITORING	• Chapter 2: Text Features and Structures, Comprehension Monitoring
	• Chapter 4: Meta Talk, Tell vs. Ask, Retrieval Practices (Brain Dump, Three Things and a Question, Learning Quiz), 5 Steps to Success, Top 3 Hits, How Am I Doing?
	• Chapter 5: Match the Picture, Get Ready/Do/Done, STOP

Brain-Boosting Learning Plan

When you approach learning experiences in brain-appealing ways, you'll get a better bang for your buck and have more fun in the process. Additionally, your students with EF challenges will pay closer attention.

With these thoughts in mind, ask yourself, "Am I aligning my teaching with how the brain likes to learn? Who's doing most of the "talking, thinking, and processing?" Remember: "Those who do the thinking do the learning!"[65]

What follows is a modified version of Willis' Neuro-logical Lesson Planner, which I call a **Brain-Boosting Learning Plan**. It's designed to decrease stress, seize children's natural curiosity, address their needs/strengths, build EF, boost engagement, promote active learning, and experience joy in the learning process.[66] Again, isn't that what we want?

As you use the plan for your lessons, incorporate as many of the aforementioned tips and strategies from the **Brain Boosters** and **Executive Function Cheat Sheets** as possible.

BRAIN-BOOSTING LEARNING PLAN

Subject: _____ Topic/Concepts:_____

Goal:_____

Objectives:_____

BRAIN-BOOSTING APPROACHES	YOUR BRAIN-BOOSTING PLAN
Getting Attention: *Which brain booster(s) will I use to get students' attention right out of the gate?*	
Buy-in: *How will I boost relevance/ value in "the learning?"*	
Motivation: *How will I take advantage of the dopamine effect?*	
Short-Term Memory: *How will I connect prior knowledge to new information?*	

BRAIN-BOOSTING APPROACHES	YOUR BRAIN-BOOSTING PLAN
Executive Function: *Check off the skills I'll reinforce in the lesson, assignment(s), or homework, and name the strategy(ies) I'll use to develop them.* ❑ **Goal Setting:** ❑ **Planning/Prioritizing:** ❑ **Organization:** ❑ **Task Initiation:** ❑ **Time Management:** ❑ **Working Memory:** ❑ **Focus:** ❑ **Effort/Mindset:** ❑ **Cognitive Flexibility:** ❑ **Response Inhibition:** ❑ **Self-Regulation:** ❑ **Self-Monitoring:**	
Classroom Culture: *How will I reduce "mistake fear" and foster a resilient and respectful community?*	
Sustaining Attention: *How will I keep students' attention?*	

BRAIN-BOOSTING APPROACHES	YOUR BRAIN-BOOSTING PLAN
Social and Emotional Learning: *How will I build SEL?*	
Achievable Challenge: *How will I differentiate instruction and reduce cognitive overload (if needed)?*	
Formative Assessments: *How will I monitor progress?* (i.e., Think-Draw-Write Pair Shares, Retrieval Strategies, Meta-Talk, Self-Monitoring)	
Feedback: *How will I give effective feedback?* (i.e., specific, objective, timely comments that focus on process and target just a few areas for improvement)	
Active Processing: *How will students boost neuroplasticity needed for long-term memory?* (i.e., ample practice, feedback implementation, and varied ways to process concepts)	
Learning/Skill Transfer: *What will I do to facilitate this?* (i.e., Bloom's Taxonomy, real-world problem-solving/projects)	

Strategies to Internalize Routines

To build productive habits and independent routines, it helps for EF strategies to "live" in your environment (i.e., class or home) so kids get regular practice internalizing important information or steps in *their* brains and eventually "own the learning."[67] The following strategies, introduced to me by Sarah Ward and Kristen Jacobsen flex kids' organization, planning, and metacognitive muscles by cuing them on how to do something instead of telling them what to do (or repeating yourself multiple times). Post these strategies on walls, anchor charts, desks, or other visible spots.

Match the Picture

What is it?
A checklist that "matches" behavior expectations to pictures and visual cues.

When to use?
Transitions, routines, class norms/procedures, task or process (i.e., organizing a desk/room, homework/sports routine).

Why use?
To help students develop a "mind map" of the expectations/steps.

How to make your own Match the Picture:

1. Decide on a routine or behavior expectation(s) you'd like your student(s) to follow. If the routine involves steps, aim for no more than five. For instance, if want your students to line up for dismissal wearing jackets and backpacks on shoulders, either show one picture that represents a student in this "finished mode" or provide a picture for each step (jacket, backpack, line up).

2. On a sheet or poster, post the image(s) that represents the "finished product" or steps.

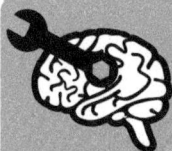

PRO TIP

Picture This!
If possible, photograph your actual student(s) doing the expected behavior(s). If that's not feasible, take a picture of yourself doing so.

When teaching this strategy, get the students doing some thinking. Here's how:

1. Pointing to your Match the Picture sheet, say, "This is what you look like when you_____" (i.e., line up for science, go to school, get ready for soccer).

2. Ask student(s) to describe the picture(s) and what they notice. If working with a group, consider a Think-Pair-Share for this step.

3. Post the sheet in a visible spot.

4. When it's time to implement the expected behavior, repeat step one and say, "Match the Picture." If kids miss something, ask them to revisit the picture(s), notice what they've done, and what still needs "matching." This helps them self-monitor their actions.

Many educators and parents find themselves repeating the same reminders every day (i.e., "Pay attention," "Grab your backpack," or "Start your homework."). Wouldn't it be wonderful if those verbal reminders worked? Unfortunately, they are a sign you've stored the steps in *your* mind, but your kids haven't…*yet*. The images below cue kids to internalize these expectations and are samples of those I've made with my students.

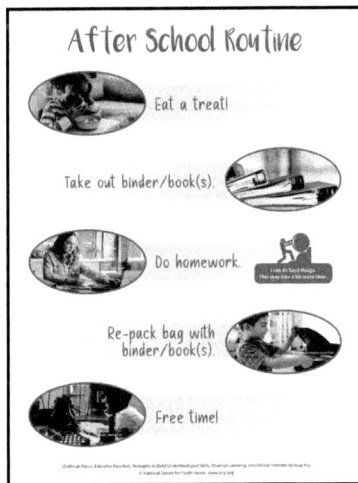

Morning Routine

- Put Your Plate in the Sink.
- Get Dressed.
- Brush Teeth and Hair.
- Put on Shoes.
- Grab Your Backpack.

After School Routine

- Eat a treat!
- Take out binder/book(s).
- Do homework.
- Re-pack bag with binder/book(s).
- Free time!

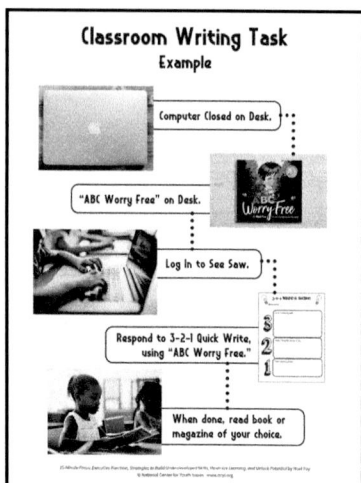

Classroom Writing Task
Example

Computer Closed on Desk.

"ABC Worry Free" on Desk.

Log In to Sea Saw.

Respond to 3-2-1 Quick Write, using "ABC Worry Free."

When done, read book or magazine of your choice.

Your Turn!

What behavior expectations or routines challenge your students? Draw a rough sketch of a Match the Picture to help students internalize this routine:

Get Ready, Do, Done

What is it?
A metacognitive workout to cue kids about the expectations and parts of a task or process from its beginning to completion.

When to use?
Homework, assignments/projects (even long-term), recipes/processes

Why use?
To make planning visible and "see" the steps, work, and expectations involved.

Here's how:

1. Start with the "DONE" box. Here's why: the far right box sends a message to the brain of seeing and stepping in to the future. In this box, sketch a rough picture of the finished work.

2. Work backward to the "DO" box, listing the steps needed to make the finished product. Estimate how long each step might take.

3. In the "GET READY" box, list or sketch what you'll need to do (or prepare) before getting started.

4. After you finish what's in the Get Ready, Do, and Done columns, complete the "Get Done" step (i.e., submit work, clean up, share on Google classroom, etc.).

Note: Model and think aloud the above steps with an example similar to what you are asking your students to do. Then, via a guided practice, involve students in the process by asking them to answer the questions in each section and fill in the chart. (If working with a group, do Pair-Shares for these questions.)

Your Turn!

What project, assignment, or process are you doing with your student(s) that lends itself to Get Ready, Do, Done?

Make a completed Get Ready, Do, Done to model with your students.

STOP Strategy

The mnemonic for this strategy stands for:

- **S**=Space
- **T**=Time
- **O**=Objects
- **P**=People

What is it?
A mnemonic with visual cues and "meta talk" that correspond to the steps and materials for a task, process, or activity.

When to use?
It's particularly helpful for transitions, especially if students need to bring specific materials. It can also help with "situational intelligence" and "reading the room."

Why use it?
To boost self-awareness, organization, focus, attention to detail, time management, prioritizing, making predictions, forethought, self-regulation, and mindset.

Here are some examples:

Teacher Story

While many of the K-12 teachers I work with realize that "eyes on them" doesn't mean their students are actually listening and learning, they (teachers) voice concerns about losing academic learning time if they implement engagement, SEL, or learning strategies into their lessons.

Through my classroom modeling of stress management strategies, "more of them, less of you" approaches, retrieval practices, and the Brain-Boosting Learning Plan, many educators have discovered that embedding these practices in their daily routines actually *saves* time! Teachers notice less stress and re-teaching and an increase in learning, work quality, and EF! Instead of students spacing out or acting out, looking straight through you, or bobbing their heads in agreement when they're actually writing songs in their heads (as one of my sons used to do), kids stay more on task by actively engaging and processing. Hearing the transfer of learning to higher levels of critical thinking is music to my ears (pun intended), as are the following outcomes teachers have shared with me when they use these strategies:

- Decreases stress, behavior problems, and repeating directions/content
- Gets more learners on the same page
- Increases attention, engagement, motivation, growth mindset, academic risk-taking, resilience, EF, and participation (particularly for those with gaps in these areas)
- Increases academic performance

As one middle school teacher shared, "I could take the lesson up a notch to gain higher, deeper, wider thinking about the content and see a transfer of the material taught. The transference for me—a HUGE

GAIN! I find these techniques offer more opportunities to engage all learners and keep all students on task. With them in the 'zone of engagement,' I can give that gradual release of independence to the students because I know these strategies promote productivity. One of the best parts is listening to students discuss their thinking in paired chats. I believe it gives them a sense of value as members in our learning community and a boost of confidence all young people need to feel empowered. In the end, these 'moves' have helped me maintain and improve a risk-taking, safe, 'kids can speak' classroom culture. We must celebrate how the learners in front of us today have so much to offer, and we need to allow them to do so. My students have improved in how they actively participate but also in how much they are truly learning—like 'real deal' authentic learning. In short, these approaches have made me a better teacher!"

1. What types of dopamine-boosting activities and practices do you consistently employ?

2. To what extent is your classroom or environment a PEE Zone?

3. In what ways can you envision using Match the Picture, Get Ready, Do, Done, and STOP?

4. How might the Brain-Boosting Learning Plan decrease stress and enhance your teaching and students' learning?

KEY POINTS

- Your brain is a pleasure-seeking organ that releases dopamine when the body does something enjoyable.

- When stress is high, dopamine drops, learning goes down, and information won't reach the thinking centers of the brain.

- A PEE Zone learning environment tends not to be "intentional" and "transparent" with strategy use and is typically low on active learning and student engagement.

- Match the Picture and Get Ready, Do, Done cue kids to match their actions to visuals of steps or behavior expectations.

- The STOP strategy cues kids with pictures and "meta talk" to build forethought and a mental schema to "read a room" or prepare for a class, process, or transition.

- The Brain-Boosting Learning Plan builds skills/knowledge and addresses needs/strengths while decreasing stress. It also promotes curiosity, creativity, engagement, active learning, EF, growth mindset, and joy in learning.

Conclusion

Kids need to know they wake up with a new brain every day because they don't come fully wired. They are still developing and can improve their skills! While EF, SEL, and EQ may not be the sexiest topics, they are essential to success, from filtering out distractions, adapting to change, and handling multiple demands to regulating emotions, working cooperatively, and becoming self-driven individuals.

As the most interconnected and stressed-out generation faces unlimited distractions and online information competing for their attention 24/7, developing strong EF is more important than ever. With the blurring of day and night, more attention and instruction are needed to teach kids *how* to juggle all the "stuff" in their lives, including how to manage their digital devices, academics, extracurriculars, social life, and well-being.[68]

Though we haven't *yet* adequately adapted instructional practices to maximize kids' EF and reflect discoveries about the brain, I believe we can make that happen! With effective training and support using the science of learning and reading, we can influence students' healthy brain and executive function development, which can boost their self-esteem, autonomy, and knowledge. We can literally change students' lives, turning their executive dysfunction into executive function—a win for them, our schools, communities, and future workforce!

I hope this book has expanded your understanding of EF, and how you as difference makers and brain changers play such a critical role. When kids have better EF, they do better in and outside of school. We have a collective responsibility to help students with unhealthy self-narratives to rewrite their story and grow into adults who are prepared to succeed at work, engage in healthy relationships, and take charge of their lives. I challenge you to see these kids with a fresh lens and provide them with transformative tools they can use in school and life. By providing them (and all kids) with quality learning environments and emotionally supportive experiences at home and school, they'll develop the EF, SEL, EQ, and critical thinking needed to meet 21st century demands, challenges, and opportunities that lie ahead.

Is this challenging work? Of course. Is it doable? Absolutely!

I yearn for kids to re-ignite their spark for school and hear them say, "Learning *how* to learn is cool!" instead of the refrain, "School is not for me." I hope this book inspires you to give them hope. Help them believe in themselves. Rekindle that spark into a flame of lifelong learning with less stress, more joy, and a path to unlocking their unique potential.

Be that kind of impact.

Endnotes

1. "The Explainer: Emotional Intelligence," Harvard Business Review, August 18, 2015, https://hbr.org/video/4421646384001/the-explainer-emotional-intelligence.

2. Russell Barkley, Ph.D., "The Important Role of Executive Functioning and Self-Regulation in ADHD," https://www.russellbarkley.org/factsheets/ADHD_EF_and_SR.pdf.

3. George McCloskey, "Executive Functions: A General Overview for Parents and Teachers," 2015, https://www.hcpss.org/f/schools/psychology/executive-functions-overview.pdf.

4. Peg Dawson and Richard Guare, *Executive Skills in Children and Adolescents: A Practical Guide to Assessment and Intervention*, (The Guildford Press, 2004).

5. Jack Naglieri and Kathleen Kryza, "How to Keep Student's Executive Function Functioning During a Pandemic: Effective Strategies for Teachers, Parents and Students," Learning and the Brain Conference Online Workshop, January 16, 2021.

6. Judy Willis, MD, MEd "Neuroscience and Executive Skills: Strategies for Executive Functions, Memory, and Classroom Learning," Santa Barbara, CA Learning and the Brain Workshop, July 28-August 1, 2014.

7. Ibid

8. Ibid

9. "Why Social and Emotional Learning is Essential for Students," Roger Weissberg, February 15, 2016, https://www.edutopia.org/blog/why-sel-essential-for-students-weissberg-durlak-domitrovich-gullotta

10. "The Impact of Enhancing Students' Social and Emotional Learning: A Meta-Analysis of School-Based Universal Interventions," Durlack et al., February 3, 2011, https://srcd.onlinelibrary.wiley.com/doi/10.1111/j.1467-8624.2010.01564.x.

11. Judy Willis, MD, MEd "Neuroscience and Executive Skills: Strategies for Executive Functions, Memory, and Classroom Learning," Santa Barbara, CA Workshop, July 28th-August 1, 2014.

12. Ibid.

13. Dr. Jack Shonkoff, Center on the Developing Child, Harvard University.

14. National Institutes of Health, "Brain Matures a Few Years Late in ADHD, But Follows Normal Pattern," November 12, 2007, https://www.nih.gov/news-events/news-releases/brain-matures-few-years-late-adhd-follows-normal-pattern

15. Jack A. Naglieri and Kathleen Kryza, "How to Keep Student's Executive Function Functioning during a Pandemic: Effective Strategies for Teachers, Parents, and Students," Learning and the Brain Conference Online Workshop January 16, 2021.

16. Journal of Psychiatry, "The Relationship between Executive Functioning and Emotional Intelligence in Children with Autism Spectrum Disorder," Volume 8, No. 3, July 2018, https://www.scirp.org/journal/paperinformation?paperid=85967

17. Adele Diamond, "Executive Functions," September 27, 2012, https://www.ncbi.nlm.nih.gov/pmc/articles/PMC4084861/

18. Kelly B. Cartwright, *Executive Skills: What are They, and Why are They Important for Developing Thinking Readers?*, Guilford Publications, 2023.

19. International Dyslexia Association, "Scarborough's Reading Rope: A Groundbreaking Infographic," Volume 7, Issue 2, April 2018, https://dyslexiaida.org/scarboroughs-reading-rope-a-groundbreaking-infographic/

20. Linda R. Hecker, M.Ed., "The Reading Brain: Executive Function Hard at Work," https://ldaamerica.org/info/the-reading-brain-executive-function-hard-at-work/

21. This is from a Keys to Literacy workshop.

22. Heather Cella, NWEA, "Why Transcription is in Your Child's Reading and Writing Journey," August 11, 2022, https://www.nwea.org/blog/2022/why-transcription-is-important-in-your-childs-writing-and-reading-journey/#:~:text=They%20have%20very%20little%20free,much%20conscious%20thought%20and%20effort.

23. Kate Kelly, "5 Ways Executive Function Can Impact Math," https://www.understood.org/en/articles/ways-executive-functioning-challenges-can-impact-math

24. Ibid.

25. Elise Franchino, "How Children's Relationships with Teachers Shape their Social-Emotional and Executive Function Skills," February 7, 2022, https://www.newamerica.org/education-policy/edcentral/how-childrens-relationships-with-teachers-shape-their-social-emotional-and-executive-function-skills/

26. Art Tuckerman, "Are You Time Blind? 12 Ways to Use Every Hour Effectively," January 21, 2023, https://www.additudemag.com/slideshows/stop-wasting-time/.

27. Barbara Oakley PhD PE and Olav Schewe, *Learn Like a Pro: Science Based Tools to Become Better at Anything*, (Essentials, June 1, 2021)

28. Sarah Kesty, "How to Get Students to Use Their Planners," Edutopia, October 11, 2022, https://www.edutopia.org/article/how-get-students-use-their-planners/#:~:text=Emphasize%20How%20Planners%20Help%20Students,sports%20games%2C%20and%20field%20trips.

29. This is from a workshop with Sarah Ward of Cognitive Connections.

30. Jessica Minahan, PhD., BCBA, *The Behavior Code Companion: Strategies, Tools, and Interventions for Supporting Students with Anxiety-Related or Oppositional Behaviors* (Harvard Education Press, 2015)

31. Ibid.

32. Crossman, Suzanne et al, "Executive Function 101," The Lantern, Fall/Winter 2017-18.

33. SMARTS, "4 Ways to Boost Executive Function When Teaching Note-Taking," https://smarts-ef.org/blog/4-ways-to-boost-executive-function-when-teaching-note-taking/

34. This is from a Keys to Literacy workshop.

35. Jessica Minahan, PhD., BCBA, "Practical Strategies for Reducing Anxiety and Challenging Behavior," Chesapeake Beach Professional Seminars Online Workshop, June 18, 2020.

36. Ibid.

37. Judy Willis MD, MEd, "Neuroscience and Executive Skills: Strategies for Executive Functions, Memory, and Classroom Learning," Santa Barbara, CA, Learning and the Brain Workshop, July 28-August 1, 2014.

38. Roy Baroody, MD, "Why Childhood Anxiety Often Goes Undetected (and the Consequences)," October 26, 2023, https://childmind.org/article/detecting-childhood-anxiety/

39. David Osher, *Less Cortisol, More Oxytocin: Achieving Educational Equity Through Social and Emotional Learning and Conditions for Learning*," American Institutes for Research, December 14, 2017, https://www.hkedcity.net/goelearning/sites/default/files/upload/5ab4b9f6903443e232020000/1521793411.92.2092810080.pdf.

40. Katie Anderson, "Teaching with Trauma in Mind," Conscious Teaching Online Workshop, March 27, 2021

41. Ibid.

42. Lynn Lyons, "Helping Children with Anxiety: Lynn Lyons Talks to Kids," 2017, https://www.youtube.com/watch?v=N7PSgsabK_I,.

43. "The Enduring Effects of Abuse and Related Adverse Experiences in Childhood," Robert F. Anda, Vincent Felitti "et al.," National Library of Medicine, November 29, 2005, https://www.ncbi.nlm.nih.gov/pmc/articles/PMC3232061/

44. Dan Siegel, "Name it to Tame it, "Dalai Lama Center for Peace and Education, December 8, 2014, https://www.youtube.com/watch?v=ZcDLzppD4Jc.

45. This is from an online workshop with Britt Andreatta, PhD.

46. Lynn Lyons on Helping Anxious Kids, 2019, "Certification Training on Clinical Child & Adolescent Treatment," PESI.

47. Carol Dweck, *Mindset, The Psychology of Success,* (Random House, 2006)

48. Ibid.

49. Kathleen Kryza, "Executive Functions and Mindset with Kathleen Kryza," 2015, https://www.youtube.com/watch?v=6s2VM6PshIM.

50. "On the Outcomes of Teacher Wellbeing: a Systematic Review of Research," Benjamin Dreer, Frontiers in Psychology, Volume 14, July 27, 2023, https://www.frontiersin.org/articles/10.3389/fpsyg.2023.1205179/full

51. Katie Anderson, "Teaching with Trauma in Mind," Conscious Teaching Online Workshop, March 27, 2021

52. This is from a Learning and the Brain Conference workshop with Kathleen Kryza.

53. Sarah Ward, MS, CCC/SLP, "The 360 Thinking Model: Practical Strategies to Improve Executive Function Skills," Learning and the Brain Online Workshop, January 27, 2024.

54. Jack Naglieri and Kathleen Kryza, "How to Keep Student's Executive Function Functioning During a Pandemic: Effective Strategies for Teachers, Parents and Students, Learning and the Brain Conference Online Workshop, January 16, 2021.

55. Sarah Ward, M.S., CCC/SLP and Kristen Jacobsen M.S., CCC/SLP, "Job Talk," Cognitive Connections, https://www.efpractice.

56. John Hattie, *Visible Learning for Teachers*, (Routledge, 1st edition, December 12, 2012)

57. Pooja K. Agarwal, Ph.D. and Patrice M. Bain, Ed.S. *Powerful Teaching*: *Unleash the Science of Learning,* (Jossey-Bass, 2019).

58. Ibid.

59. Lynn Meltzer, Research Institute for Learning and Development, SMARTS Executive Function Workshop "How to Integrate EF Strategies in Your Teaching," Boston, MA, February 2, 2018.

60. "thinkSMARTer. Not Harder: Understanding Executive Function from Brain to Behaviors," Alisa J. Ellis, Ph.D., https://www.thehelpgroup.org/thinksmarter-not-harder-understanding-executive-functions-from-brains-to-behaviors/

61. How do We Know When Students Are Engaged?" Ben Johnson, Updated November 2, 2013, https://www.edutopia.org/blog/student-engagement-definition-ben-johnson

62. Judy Willis, MD, MEd, *How Your Child Learns Best: Brain-Friendly Strategies You Can Use to Ignite Your Child's Learning and Increase School Success* (Sourcebooks Inc., 2008).

63. Ibid.

64. Judy Willis , MD, Med, "Neuroscience and Executive Skills: Strategies for Executive Functions, Memory, and Classroom Learning," Santa Barbara, CA, Learning and the Brain Workshop, July 28th-August 1, 2014.

65. Ibid.

66. Ibid.

67. Sarah Ward, MS, CCC/SLP, "The 360 Thinking Model: Practical Strategies to Improve Executive Function Skills," Learning and the Brain Online Workshop, January 27, 2024.

68. David Allen, Mike Williams, and Mark Wallace, *Getting Things Done for Teens: Take Control of Your Life in a Distracting World* (Penguin Books, 2018)

Resources

Websites

EXECUTIVE FUNCTION

- https://www.efpractice.com — support, tools, and resources for kids/adults
- https://smarts-ef.org — executive function curriculum and resources for educators/families
- https://jacknaglieri.com — resources for educators/counselors
- https://kathleenkryza.com — support and resources for educators/families
- https://radteach.com — resources and tips for educators/families
- https://www.russellbarkley.org/newsletter.html — ADHD Report Newsletter
- https://www.schoolhouseeducationalservices.com/mccloskey-executive-functions-scale-mefs/ — EF assessment
- https://kellycartwright.com/books-%26-handouts — talks and downloads
- https://developingchild.harvard.edu/?s=executive+function — research and support
- http://www.devcogneuro.com — Adele Diamond's Developmental Cognitive Neuroscience Lab
- https://childmind.org — resources and support on SEL/neurodiversity/mental health

ADHD

- https://www.cdc.gov — key points, diagnosis, treatment
- https://www.brownadhdclinic.com/the-brown-model-of-add-adhd — symptoms of ADHD
- https://chadd.org — information and support for parents/educators
- https://www.additudemag.com — resources for families
- https://www.ldonline.org — resources on learning disabilities/ADHD
- https://drhallowell.com — diagnosis and treatment

SOCIAL AND EMOTIONAL LEARNING

- www.casel.com — Collaborative for Social and Emotional Learning
- https://www.classdojo.com — video series
- https://home.mindup.org — SEL curriculum/trainings for teachers PreK-8, including mindfulness, neuroscience, and positive psychology
- www.responsibleclassroom.org — SEL approach to teaching and discipline
- https://www.toolsofthemind.org — early childhood self-regulation activities

BEHAVIOR

- https://jessicaminahan.com — Jessica Minahan, behavioral analyst specializing in articles and workshops for educators, parents, and counselors
- https://behaviorqueen.com — Amie Dean, behavioral expert with workshops and resources on classroom behavior interventions

ANXIETY

- www.lynnlyons.com — Lynn Lyons, psychotherapist specializing in supporting anxious families
- https://drlisadamour.com — Lisa Damour, psychologist and author specializing in supporting families of teenagers, particularly girls and those with anxiety
- www.neuronoel.com — my website, specializing in supporting schools, families, and organizations with workshops, one-on-one coaching, and author visits on anxiety and executive function

MINDFULNESS

- https://www.drchristopherwillard.com — psychologist with resources/ videos on mindfulness

WRITING AND COMPREHENSION

- https://keystoliteracy.com — literacy training and resources on reading/ writing skills

Videos

BRAIN, NEUROPLASTICITY, AND EXECUTIVE FUNCTION

- https://www.youtube.com/watch?v=ELpfYCZa87g — Sentis Video — Neuroplasticity and Brain Animation Series
- https://www.youtube.com/watch?v=g7FdMi03CzI — Kizoom — *Brain Jump with Ned the Neuron: Challenges Grow Your Brain*
- https://www.youtube.com/watch?v=CiHeMO9IGvE — ClassDojo — video series on the brain, growth mindset, and social and emotional learning
- https://www.youtube.com/watch?v=6s2VM6PshIM — Kathleen Kryza — *Executive Function and Mindset*
- https://www.youtube.com/watch?v=efCq_vHUMqs —Center on the Developing Child, Harvard University — *Executive Function: Skills for Life and Learning*
- https://www.youtube.com/watch?v=BKb51xq-eWA — Neuroscience News — *Childhood Stress' Long-Term Effect on Brain*

GROWTH MINDSET

- https://www.youtube.com/watch?v=hiiEeMN7vbQ — Carol Dweck
- https://www.youtube.com/watch?v=W3FCbP8rdRU — Michael Jordon
- https://www.youtube.com/watch?v=zLYECIjmnQs — Famous Failures

ANXIETY

- https://www.youtube.com/watch?v=4B_4V5Mz5Ho — ABC Strategy —how to manage anxiety

BREATHING TECHNIQUES

- https://www.youtube.com/watch?v=1xbXYj8rnCc — 3 Quick Breathing Techniques to Calm and Reset

Articles/Blogs

EXECUTIVE FUNCTION / ADHD / NEURODIVERSITY

- https://smarts-ef.org/blog/
- https://www.ncbi.nlm.nih.gov/pmc/articles/PMC4084861/

- https://www.hcpss.org/f/schools/psychology/executive-functions-overview.pdf
- https://www.russellbarkley.org/factsheets/ADHD_EF_and_SR.pdf
- https://children.wi.gov/Documents/Harvard%20Parenting%20Resource.pdf
- https://d393uh8gb46l22.cloudfront.net/wp-content/uploads/2018/06/ATTN_02_08_School_Success_by_Chris_Dendy.pdf
- https://www.landmarkschool.org/our-school/landmark-360-blog?id=253207/executive-function-101
- https://www.nih.gov/news-events/news-releases/brain-matures-few-years-late-adhd-follows-normal-pattern
- https://www.edutopia.org/article/5-ways-help-neurodiverse-students-improve-executive-function-skills/
- https://www.additudemag.com/executive-function-adhd-kids-lagging-skills/#:~:text=A%20child%20with%20ADHD%20has,EF%20age%20is%20about%2016 (what parents might misunderstand)
- https://www.understood.org/en/articles/9-tips-for-talking-to-your-childs-teacher-about-executive-function-challenges

TIME AND PLANNING TOOLS

- https://www.additudemag.com/slideshows/stop-wasting-time/
- https://www.edutopia.org/article/how-get-students-use-their-planners/

READING

- https://ldaamerica.org/info/the-reading-brain-executive-function-hard-at-work/#:~:text=EF%20integrates%20and%20synchronizes%20the,prior%20knowledge%20with%20new%20information

MATH

- https://prek-math-te.stanford.edu/overview/overview-executive-functioning-and-math
- https://preschoolmath.stanford.edu/toolkit/what-are-executive-function-skills-and-how-are-they-related-to-math/

WRITING

- https://www.nwea.org/blog/2022/why-transcription-is-important-in-your-childs-writing-and-reading-j

SEL

- https://www.edutopia.org/blog/why-sel-essential-for-students-weissberg-durlak-domitrovich-gullotta
- https://www2.ed.gov/documents/students/supporting-child-student-social-emotional-behavioral-mental-health.pdf

TEACHER TALK

- https://www.edutopia.org/article/limit-teacher-talk-increase-student-engagement-achievement/
- https://www.edutopia.org/article/talk-less-so-students-learn-more/

Podcasts

- www.flusterclux — Fix Anxiety with Lynn Lyons — parent tips on anxiety
- https://drlisadamour.com/resources/podcast/ — Ask Lisa — parents tips on teens/anxiety
- https://drhallowell.com/listen/podcast/ — Wonderful Word of Different — stories of overcoming obstacles for all kinds of minds
- https://www.candyoterry.com/post/noel-foy — The Story Behind Her Success — I discuss anxiety, executive function, and neurodiversity.
- https://podcasters.spotify.com/pod/show/american-institute-of-stress/episodes/Stress-Effects-in-Children-What-Teachers-and-Parents-Need-to-Know-ef6j35 — "Finding Contentment," The American Institute of Stress podcast — I discuss stress' impact on learning.

Tools

EXECUTIVE FUNCTION

- https://www.inspiration.com — Inspiration — visual mapping software
- Visual Countdown Analog Clock — 60-minute visual timer with countdown
- https://us.livescribe.com — Smart Pen — records what you write, hear, or say and sends it to tablet or smartphone
- https://notability.com — organize/record/share/replay notes and annotate PDF's

Apps

EXECUTIVE FUNCTION

- https://chromewebstore.google.com/detail/forest-stay-focused-be-pr/kjacjjdnoddnpbbcjilcajfhhbdhkpgk — self-motivating approach to decrease phone use/browsing, internet addiction, and improve focus/time management
- https://www.beelinereader.com — color gradient pulls eyes through texts to boost focus/reading efficiency
- https://chromewebstore.google.com/detail/postlight-reader/oknpjjbmpnndlpmnhmekjpocelpnlfdi?hl=en — removes ads from online articles

Books

- *How Your Child Learns Best* (Bridgepoint Education Inc., 2014) — Judy Willis
- *Helping Children Learn: Intervention Handouts for Use at School and Home* (Baltimore, MD: Brookes Publishing, 2010, 2nd edition) — J. A. Naglieri and E. B Pickering
- *Promoting Executive Function in the Classroom* (New York: Guilford Press, 2018, 2nd ed.) — Meltzer, L.J. (Ed.)
- *The Anxiety Audit* (Simon & Schuster, 2022) — Lynn Lyons
- *Visible Learning: The Sequel, A Synthesis of Over 2,100 Meta-Analyses Relating to Achievement* (Routledge, 2023) — John Hattie
- *Developing Growth Mindset in the Inspiring Classroom* Grades K-12 (Inspiring Learners, Inc, 2016) — Kathleen Kryza
- *Mindset, The Psychology of Success* (Random House, 2006) — Carol Dweck
- *The Behavior Code Companion: Strategies, Tools, and Interventions for Supporting Students with Anxiety-Related or Oppositional Behaviors* (Harvard Education Press, 2015) — Jessica Minahan
- *Smart But Scattered: The Revolutionary "Executive Skills" Approach to Helping Kids Reach Their Potential*, (Guilford Press, 2009) — Peg Dawson and Richard Guare
- *Treating ADHD in Children and Adolescents: What Every Clinician Needs to Know* (The Guildford Press, 2022) — Russell A. Barkley, Ph.D.

- *Learn Like a Pro, Science-Based Tools to Become Better at Anything* (St. Martin's Publishing Group, 2021) — Barbara Oakley, PHD, PE and Olav Schewe
- *Powerful Teaching, Unleash the Science of Learning* (Jossey-Bass, 2019) — Pooja K. Agarwal, Ph.D. and Patrice M. Bain, Ed.S.
- *Getting Things Done for Teens: Take Control of Your Life in a Distracting World* (Penguin Books, 2018) — David Allen, Mike Williams, Mark Wallace
- *The Body Keeps the Score, Brain, Mind, and Body in the Healing of Trauma* (Penguin Books, 2015) — Bessel van der Kolk
- *The Key Comprehension Routine:* Grades 4-12 (3rd edition, 2015) — Joan Sedita
- *Keys to Content Writing* (4th edition, 2020) — Joan Sedita
- *Executive Skills and Reading Comprehension: A Guide for Educators*, Second Edition (Guilford Press, 2023) — Kelly B. Cartwright
- *Light Up the Learning Brain: 7 Keys to Reducing Disruptive Behavior in the Classroom* (National Center for Youth Issues, 2024) — Jessica Sinarski
- *The Self-Driven Child: The Science and Sense of Giving Your Kids More Control Over Their Lives*, (Viking Press, 2018) — William Stixrud, PhD and Ned Johnson
- *Spark: The Revolutionary New Science of Exercise and the Brain* (Little Brown, 2013) —Jack Ratey
- *I Can't find My Whatchamacallit!* (National Center for Youth Issues, 2015) — Julia Cook

E-Book

- *Pass Theory of Intelligence and the CAS2* by Jack Naglieri and Tulio M. Otero

Acknowledgements

For my husband — my partner and best friend. I am forever grateful for you.

For my sons, daughters-in-law, and grandchildren — You are my "why." I've learned and grown so much by having you in my life. Thank you for your love, patience, feedback, endless encouragement, and for filling my cup with joy.

For Jennifer — Thank you for believing in me and this book, even when things got tricky! Your impact on children, families, educators, and support for professionals is immeasurable.

For the educators, counselors, students, parents, and professionals I've had the privilege of working with — you inspire me to take my game to a higher level, and I hope I do the same for you!

DOWNLOADABLE RESOURCES

The resources in this book are available to you as a digital download!

Please visit **15minutefocusseries.com** and click this book cover on the page. Once you've clicked the book cover, a prompt will ask you for a code to unlock the activities.

Please enter code:

ExecFun567

About the Author

NOEL FOY is a mom, grandmother, former teacher, and learning specialist who evolved into a neuroeducational consultant, anxiety/executive function coach, and author.

Commonly known as Neuro Noel, she transforms neuroscience findings into practical applications to reduce the impact of stress on learning and appeal to how the brain learns best. Traditional teaching practices often omit this critical focus and fall short of meeting the needs of many students, resulting in gaps in learning and executive function and an increase in behavioral issues or not reaching one's true potential.

Via workshops, one-on-one coaching, author visits, and speaking engagements, Noel equips schools, families, and professionals with a toolbox of practical language, responses, and applications that lower stress and build underdeveloped skills sets and mindsets needed to maximize success and experience life-changing outcomes.

Additionally, Noel finds storytelling an approachable and playful way to tackle complex topics. Her books encourage productive change and the will to face fears through courage and friendship.

Other Books By Noel

ABC Worry Free

Max's worries hold him back from playing with friends and doing what he loves most, until he learns how to manage his anxiety with the ABC trick.

Are You a Bird Like Me?

(with co-author Nicholas Roberto)

After a hatchling named Sky falls out of her nest, she sets out to find her parents and learns about kindness, courage, diversity, and the amazing things that happen by working together.

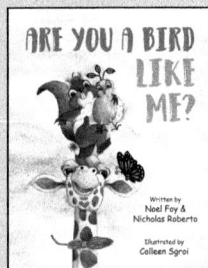

A Brief Look At Noel's Sessions

How to Build Underdeveloped Skills, Maximize Learning, and Unlock Potential

Frustrated by your disorganized and easily distracted students or those who fall apart when they encounter obstacles or challenges? How about those who have difficulty getting started, self-regulating, or remembering what they need to do? For students with executive dysfunction, school can be a hard and stressful place where they don't feel successful, but it doesn't have to stay that way.

In this interactive workshop, you'll learn practical language, responses, and applications that lower stress and build underdeveloped skill sets and mindsets needed to maximize success in school, relationships, jobs, and life. Using *15 Minute Focus: Executive Function, How to Build Underdeveloped Skills, Maximize Learning, and Unlock Potential*, we will address:

- the impact of executive dysfunction and stress
- how to use quick, practical strategies to support: goal setting, transitions, routines, organization, working memory, planning, time management, self-regulation, and self-monitoring
- how to use neuroscience and simple, learning-focused strategies to decrease stress and behavior issues while maximizing metacognition, engagement, and autonomy

Witness the powerful transformation in your students as they become empowered, efficient learners with greater motivation, resilience, and confidence!

What Anxiety Wants vs. What Anxiety Needs

With approximately a third of students qualifying for an anxiety disorder, educators and parents need a toolkit of quick and actionable strategies to use in "real time" to combat anxiety's contagious effect. Without such toolbox, your words and responses may *inadvertently* feed anxiety.

If you teach, parent, or coach kids with anxiety and wonder what to say and do to help, this interactive workshop is for you. Using *ABC Worry Free* as a reference tool, you will learn about anxiety's do's and don'ts as well as:

- How anxiety works
- Patterns of anxiety
- Myths and misunderstandings
- Communication and skill building tips

ncyionline.org/speakers

15-minute focus
Brief Counseling Techniques that Work

Look for these books in the series!

REGULATION AND CO-REGULATION
Accessible Neuroscience and Connection
Strategies that Bring Calm into the Classroom

Ginger Healy

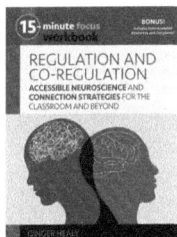

REGULATION AND CO-REGULATION WORKBOOK
Accessible Neuroscience and Connection
Strategies for the Classroom and Beyond

Ginger Healy

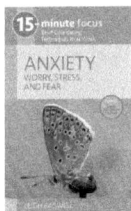

ANXIETY
Worry, Stress, and Fear

Dr. Leigh Bagwell

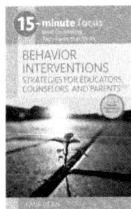

ANXIETY WORKBOOK
Tips and Strategies to manage Anxiety, Build
Resilience, and Foster Emotional Well-Being

Dr. Leigh Bagwell

BEHAVIOR INTERVENTIONS
Strategies for Educators,
Counselors, and Parents

Amie Dean

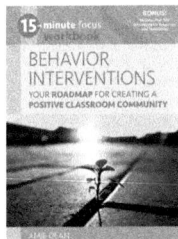

BEHAVIOR INTERVENTIONS WORKBOOK
Your Roadmap for Creating a
Positive Classroom Community

Amie Dean

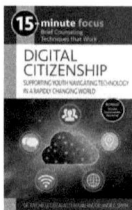

DIGITAL CITIZENSHIP
Supporting Youth Navigating
Technology in a Rapidly
Changing World

Dr. Raychelle Cassada Lohmann
and Dr. Angie Smith

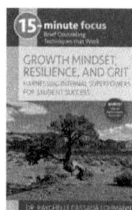

GROWTH MINDSET,
RESILIENCE, AND GRIT
Harnessing Internal Superpowers
for Student Success

Dr. Raychelle Cassada Lohmann

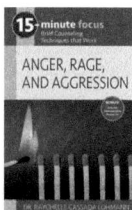

ANGER, RAGE, AND AGGRESSION

Dr. Raychelle Cassada Lohmann

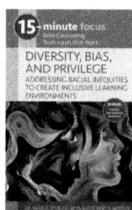

DIVERSITY, BIAS, AND PRIVILEGE
Addressing Racial Inequities
to Create Inclusive Learning
Environments

Dr. Natalie Spencer Gwyn
and Robert B. Jamison

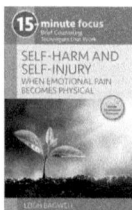

SELF-HARM AND SELF-INJURY
When Emotional Pain
Becomes Physical

Dr. Leigh Bagwell

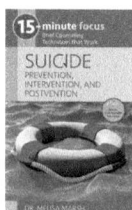

SUICIDE
Prevention, Intervention,
and Postvention

Dr. Melisa Marsh

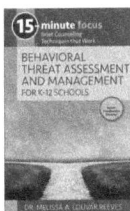

**BEHAVIORAL THREAT
ASSESSMENT AND MANAGEMENT
for K-12 Schools**

Dr. Melissa A. Louvar Reeves

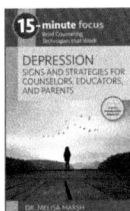

**TRAUMA
and Adverse Childhood
Experiences**

Dr. Melissa A. Louvar Reeves

**DEPRESSION
Signs and Strategies for
Counselors,
Educators, and Parents**

Dr. Melisa Marsh

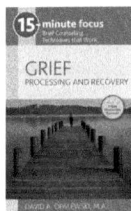

**GRIEF
Processing and Recovery**

David A. Opalewski, M.A.

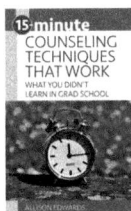

**15-MINUTE COUNSELING
TECHNIQUES THAT WORK
What You Didn't Learn
in Grad School**

Allison Edwards

NATIONAL CENTER for
YOUTH ISSUES

About NCYI

National Center for Youth Issues provides educational resources, training, and support programs to foster the healthy social, emotional, and physical development of children and youth. Since our founding in 1981, NCYI has established a reputation as one of the country's leading providers of teaching materials and training for counseling and student-support professionals. NCYI helps meet the immediate needs of students throughout the nation by ensuring those who mentor them are well prepared to respond across the developmental spectrum.

Connect With Us Online!

@nationalcenterforyouthissues

@ncyi

@nationalcenterforyouthissues